Nuclear Deterrence in Europe

Russian Approaches to a New Environment and Implications for the United States

T0150147

James T. Quinlivan, Olga Oliker

Prepared for the United States Air Force

PROJECT AIR FORCE

The research described in this report was sponsored by the United States Air Force under Contract FA7014-06-C-0001. Further information may be obtained from the Strategic Planning Division, Directorate of Plans, Hq USAF.

Library of Congress Control Number: 2011934862

ISBN: 978-0-8330-5214-8

Published 2011 by the RAND Corporation
1776 Main Street, P.O. Box 2138, Santa Monica, CA 90407-2138
1200 South Hayes Street, Arlington, VA 22202-5050
4570 Fifth Avenue, Suite 600, Pittsburgh, PA 15213-2665
RAND URL: http://www.rand.org/
To order RAND documents or to obtain additional information, contact
Distribution Services: Telephone: (310) 451-7002;
Fax: (310) 451-6915; Email: order@rand.org

Preface

This monograph examines how U.S. Air Force strategic forces contribute to and are affected by the evolving relationship with Russia. This study starts with the recognition that the simple numbers and destructive power of both countries' nuclear arsenals continue to drive at least a baseline requirement to deter the other, even though no adversarial intent exists on either side. In other important ways, however, the interests that the two sides are claiming, protecting, or advancing have changed profoundly from those of the Cold War. The American forces that constituted "deterrence" during the Cold War were matched to a vision of how conflict could come about—primarily in Europe—and how that conflict would be conducted. Changed interests and, thus, changed ways in which interests diverge mean that these visions necessarily no longer hold, although Europe remains a consistent region of concern to both countries. To effectively incorporate deterrence in the context of the current relationship with Russia, in which both sides profess not to see the other as an adversary, we must understand how both Russia and the United States might envision conflict emerging and progressing.

The Air Force has always had a special role in understanding the possible use of nuclear weapons in any conflict. This monograph looks at whether and how the possible Russian use of such weapons in the particular context of conflict escalation in a Europe or near-Europe scenario might evolve. If nuclear weapons are employed in the future, they will be employed in different ways from what might have been expected in the past—which means that the mechanisms needed to avert such developments are similarly new. The implications for the Air

Force extend beyond those formally charged with the stewardship of nuclear weapons.

The research reported here is one component of the fiscal year 2009 Assessing Options for U.S. Nuclear Forces and Arms Control study. The information in the monograph has been updated to include results of Russian exercises through 2009 and early 2010 and relevant literature through September 2010. The study was sponsored by the Strategic Deterrence and Nuclear Integration Office (AF/A10) and Plans and Requirements (AF/A5) and conducted within the Strategy and Doctrine Program of RAND Project AIR FORCE.

RAND Project AIR FORCE

RAND Project AIR FORCE (PAF), a division of the RAND Corporation, is the U.S. Air Force's federally funded research and development center for studies and analyses. PAF provides the Air Force with independent analyses of policy alternatives affecting the development, employment, combat readiness, and support of current and future aerospace forces. Research is conducted in four programs: Force Modernization and Employment; Manpower, Personnel, and Training; Resource Management; and Strategy and Doctrine.

Additional information about PAF is available on our website: http://www.rand.org/paf/

Contents

Figures and Tables

Figures

Tables

Summary

The Cold War is over, but its legacy lingers in both the United States and Russia as the two countries continue to shape and define their current and future relationship. Among the positive ways in which this relationship differs from that of the past is both sides' genuine belief that they no longer face one another as perpetual adversaries on constant guard against an opponent willing to use nuclear weapons. Within their new relationship, they are prepared to draw down the strategic nuclear forces that defined the central hostility of the Cold War. And yet, within this relationship there is still a nonviolent, but real, conflict of interests as Russia struggles to come back from its period of weakness and assert great-power status.

Looking back, the deterrent framework established by the Soviet Union and the United States comprised clearly stated vital interests and the deployment of large numbers of conventional and nuclear weapons. Through presidential statements, formal alliances, and military deployments, the United States and the Soviet Union extended deterrence to include their North Atlantic Treaty Organization (NATO) allies and Eastern European allies, respectively. Military doctrine was written and exercises were undertaken to demonstrate the capacity of the weapon systems.

Using these same elements, this monograph focuses on uncovering the characteristics of Russia's emerging deterrent framework beyond central strategic nuclear deterrence. (See Table S.1.)

Russia has made clear that, given its conventional inferiority to plausible adversaries, including the United States and NATO, it might be forced to use nuclear weapons in response to a conventional attack

Table S.1
Analytic Framework and Examination of Current Russian Deterrent Policy

Framework Element	Russian Policy and Actions
Authoritative statement of claimed interests	Russia claims privileged status in neighboring countries under the Medvedev Doctrine.
Military doctrine and practice	Military policy and past doctrine recognize that local conflicts can draw other states into regional conflicts that might pit Russian forces against NATO or American forces who will win unless Russia resorts to first use of nuclear weapons to "de-escalate military actions."
	Current published doctrine indicates that Russia will not consider the use of nuclear weapons except in the case of a weapons-of-mass-destruction threat to Russia or its allies or a conventional threat to the existence of the Russian state, leaving the question of what level or form of escalation could create such a threat.
Force development and posture	Current and near-term Russian forces reflect a focus on preparing ground forces for local conflicts rather than seeking to replicate American capabilities for "sixth-generation" warfare (i.e., employment of advanced conventional weapons, automated control systems, radio-electronic combat, precision strike, and weapons based on new physical principles). Russian retirement of legacy strategic nuclear programs represents a change from the past theory of stability, embodied in the Strategic Arms Reduction Treaty (START) program and founded on retiring multiple independently targetable reentry vehicle (MIRV) missile systems. ICBMs continue to be the privileged leg of the triad. Given current trends and START counting rules, Russia may be moving toward a lopsided, ICBM-heavy force structure.
Major exercises and scenarios	Large military exercises, used during the Cold War both to rehearse war plans and to communicate political resolve to one's adversary, have had a revival. To the extent that these exercises are presented publicly, since 1999 they have considered the case of local conflicts growing to regional wars with intervention by highly capable Western forces and eventual Russian recourse to nuclear weapons. Over time, the number of types of strategic systems that appear in such exercises has broadened—whether their purpose is to demonstrate a range of capabilities to observers or to showcase particular systems or services for internal resource decisions is unclear. In late September 2009, the Zapad-2009 exercise modeled a large-scale air and ground attack on Belarus, but it is unclear whether nuclear use was played in the exercise. In mid-2010, Vostok-2010 presented a scenario of battling illegal nonstate actors with tanks, warships, and fighter aircraft—as well as possibly a nuclear mine.
Endorsement of doctrine, forces, and exercises by political authorities	Reversing the political-military estrangement of the Yeltsin administration, Presidents Vladimir Putin and Dmitry Medvedev endorsed military doctrines that allowed for first use of nuclear weapons and conspicuously endorsed military exercises that included launch of strategic systems through 2009. In 2010, Medvedev endorsed the new doctrine and appeared at the Vostok-2010 exercise, but he has been less visible in explaining the meaning of exercises and any connections to the use of nuclear weapons. At the same time, Medvedev has been more visible internationally in support of new arms control agreements.

by such adversaries on Russia or its allies. Moreover, in asserting its power and making claims for its regional interests, Russia seeks to dissuade the United States and its NATO allies from expanding into regions where Russia claims interests and to deter unilateral U.S. or NATO intervention in the event of local conflict. In the past, recognizing conventional inferiority to the United States and NATO has led Russia to imply the potential for first use of nuclear weapons in this context, although Russia's most recent doctrine appears to walk back from that formulation. These discussions raised the possibility of nuclear weapon use that did not involve large intercontinental exchanges or preemptive nuclear strikes. Rather, limited nuclear strikes using bombers, intercontinental ballistic missiles (ICBMs), and non-strategic nuclear weapons (tactical nuclear weapons lack the range for such strikes, and intermediate-range nuclear weapons are prohibited by treaty) were envisaged.

However, Russia's new military doctrine, adopted in February 2010, declares nuclear weapon use to be limited to situations in which an adversary threatens Russia or its allies with nuclear or other weapons of mass destruction or situations in which a conventionally armed enemy threatens Russia's very existence. This suggests that Russia's leadership has made a decision to preclude the use of nuclear weapons as described above. This somewhat contradicts past statements, including those made by Russian officials before the doctrine was announced, regarding Russia's intentions.

The new doctrine leaves Russia's privileged interests unchanged; it simply raises questions as to how they will be defended, and under what circumstances. In seeking to both dissuade expansion and deter military intervention in peripheral conflicts in which Russia is involved, Russia faces the challenge of communicating its interests and intentions to other states and gaining support within its own political and military apparatus for the policies envisaged. While this new framework inherits legacy forces, programs, and elements of military doctrine from the Soviet Union, they are being shaped, changed, and, in some cases, discarded to adapt to Russia's new environment and purposes. Russia's evolving deterrent framework does not encompass the whole of Russian policy or strategy, but it is a recognizable new element that is noticeably different from the past and appears to still be in flux. Russia's deterrent framework should be taken as part of Russia's reassertion of great-power status, its views of its relationship with the United States, and its evolving position on the role of nuclear weapons in its security planning.

In considering how to respond to Russia's claims of interest in its bordering states and its opposition to further NATO expansion, the United States must make judgments about Russia's likely views and actions. While a number of other strategic considerations must also inform these decisions, decisionmakers and planners were faced, prior to the publication of the February 2010 doctrine, with the possibility that, in the absence of formally or informally recognizing these Russian interests, the United States could be drawn into a conflict that could escalate to Russian use of nuclear weapons. Such a possibility seemed not to be captured fully by existing NATO or American planning or declaratory policy. In the context of the new doctrine—because of the disconnects between the new doctrine and past exercises and evident policy directions—and absent further clarification, U.S. and U.S. Air Force decisionmakers cannot be fully confident about precisely under what circumstances Russia will consider using nuclear weapons, or what sort of nuclear use it might consider.

Prior to the publication of the February 2010 military doctrine, it would have been reasonable to argue that, to avoid having to decide in the moment whether they are prepared to respond with nuclear weapons and what weapons might be used, the United States and NATO would need to undertake planning for the changed military environment and geography in Europe. This would require an awareness of what sorts of actions and operations raise the risk of a Russian nuclear response or action, and planning accordingly so as to minimize that risk. In some cases, this would suggest avoiding certain actions and operations; in others, it might require more explicit and direct communication with Russia in planning and preoperational stages than might otherwise be deemed necessary, in order to prevent misunderstandings and misperceived signals (or actions erroneously viewed as signals) on both sides. It would also raise the adequacy of dual-capable aircraft (DCA) as the sole surviving element of in-theater nuclear forces. In the face of the new doctrine, there may be less call to worry about possible nuclear exchanges with Russia, except in circumstances where Russia feels that its existence, or that of an ally or allies, is at risk. However, recognition of Russia's interests, consideration of what responses it considers adequate short of nuclear use, and improvement of communication protocols remain called for.

There are also benefits to considering the implications of Russia's new stated nuclear doctrine in the context of its evolving force structure. Stability based on past arms control constructs (START) and on signaling with strategic nuclear bombers to promote intrawar deterrence will need rethinking, given Russian ICBM and submarine-launched ballistic missile (SLBM) force developments, as well as prospective reductions in strategic nuclear weapons under the new START agreement. Future arms control negotiations can usefully take these issues into account. Retaining the Intermediate-Range Nuclear Force (INF) Treaty needs to be a critical U.S. goal, given that a denunciation would make available more nuclear weapons in situations the United States is trying to prevent. Similarly, existing understandings on the exchange of information on long-range nuclear sea-launched cruise missiles (SLCMs) at least give some bounds on the possible size and, presumably, origin of nuclear attacks based on SLCMs.

In the meantime, Russian policymakers and analysts continue to emphasize the strategic deterrence mission of their country's nuclear arsenal and to raise concerns that U.S. missile defense programs do or will undermine Russia's capacity to deter a U.S. nuclear strike. This discussion revives fears and assertions made during the "Star Wars" era and revisits some of the same proposed responses, such as launch on warning. However, key elements of the command and control and early missile launch warning systems that would support such a response have not been modernized nor given priority attention.

From the perspective of the U.S. Air Force, there are a number of implications of Russia's evolving doctrine:

1. During the Cold War, one contribution of the Air Force was the development of a cadre of officers with deep understanding of the Soviets as a military opponent. This expertise was based on

extensive experience and study. In any situation in Europe that involves, or risks developing into, conflict with the Russians, there will be a need for this deep knowledge and an ability to inform senior political and military leadership on "what comes next" as situations develop.

2. As the principal component of the American ability to wage "contactless war," in which precision-strike assets destroy ground-based forces, the Air Force should expect that any Air Force operations against Russian forces must be planned and conducted in light of at least the possibility of Russian nuclear use.

3. Operations under a nuclear shadow demand that the Air Force not deploy for European operations in predictable patterns that present an adversary perceived opportunities to remove what it might interpret as threats to the survival of the state (its own or an ally's) with small nuclear attacks that promise both definite effects on the battlefield and "de-escalation of military actions."

4. Any actions in Europe to support American operations elsewhere have been and will be observed by a Russian military more interested in us than we are in it. It is critical that operational planning take this into account and that planners and operators take steps to prevent Russia from mistaking operations and actions as unintended "signals."

5. Nuclear systems based in the continental United States are becoming more important for any theater nuclear roles.

Acknowledgments

This project has benefited from multiple interactions and conversations with many in the Air Force community charged with reinvigorating the Air Force nuclear enterprise, including Lt Gen Frank Klotz, Lt Gen Robert Elder (Ret.), Maj Gen Donald Alston, Col Mike Shoults, Col Kirk Fansher, Col Stephen Lucky, Charles Henderson, and James Blackwell. In addition, the work benefited from dialog with the RAND program director who initiated this work, David Ochmanek, and our RAND colleagues, David Mosher, Lowell Schwartz, Roger Molander, and David Frelinger. Lynn Davis revised a first draft of this document to greatly sharpen the final monograph. David Aaron and Jacob W. Kipp reviewed an earlier draft and provided helpful suggestions on how to improve our arguments. Caroline Reilly prepared the range maps that demonstrate the new military geography and range scale for Europe.

Abbreviations

ABM   antiballistic missile

ACLM   air-launched cruise missile

CFE   Conventional Armed Forces in Europe (Treaty)

CONUS   continental United States

DCA   dual-capable aircraft

HEO   highly elliptical orbit

ICBM   intercontinental ballistic missile

INF   Intermediate-Range Nuclear Force (Treaty)

MIRV   multiple independently targetable reentry vehicle

NATO   North Atlantic Treaty Organization

ODS   Operation Desert Storm

OSCE   Organization for Security and Co-operation in Europe

OTNW   operational-tactical nuclear weapon

RV   reentry vehicle

SLBM   submarine-launched ballistic missile

SLCM   sea-launched cruise missile

SNW   strategic nuclear weapon

SORT   Strategic Offensive Reductions Treaty (better known as the Moscow Treaty)

SRF	Strategic Rocket Forces (also known as the Strategic Missile Forces)
SSBN	strategic submarine ballistic—nuclear (nuclear ballistic missile submarine)
START	Strategic Arms Reduction Treaty
TLAM-N	Tomahawk land attack missile—nuclear
TVD	*teatr voennykh deistvii* (theater of military action or operations)

CHAPTER ONE

Introduction

Starting with the end of the American nuclear monopoly in 1949, two nuclear-armed adversaries labored to produce nuclear weapons as protection for their interests and their existence in the face of their opponent's apparently implacable hostility. Harnessed within "deterrent" strategies, the large nuclear arsenals of the Cold War were the ultimate insurance policies for balance-of-force politics between the two blocs from 1949 until the demise of the Soviet Union. While deterrence and its nuclear underpinnings seemed an undoubted success in the Cold War context, after the fall of the Soviet Union former Secretary of State Henry Kissinger summed up some of the doubts that always troubled those who sought to direct the practice in the moment rather than analyze it in retrospect:

> The Nuclear Age turned strategy into deterrence, and deterrence into an esoteric intellectual exercise. Since deterrence can only be tested negatively, by events that do not take place, and since it is never possible to demonstrate why something has not occurred, it became especially difficult to assess whether the existing policy was the best possible policy or a just barely effective one. Perhaps deterrence was even unnecessary because it was impossible to prove whether the adversary ever intended to attack in the first place. Such imponderables caused domestic and international debates on nuclear matters to run the gamut from pacifism to intransigence, from paralyzing doubt to an exorbitant sense of

power, and from unproveable theories of defense to undemon-strable theories of arms control.[1]

Since the end of the Cold War, with the complete elimination of ideologically predetermined grounds of conflict, the departure of large conventional forces from the East-West border, and extensive reductions of their nuclear forces, both the United States and Russia have wrestled with whether nuclear weapons are still useful tools for deterrence. In successive policy documents (particularly the U.S. nuclear posture reviews and Russia's national security strategies and military doctrines), both countries appear to have decided that nuclear deterrence continues to serve a purpose, although their views of who is to be deterred, and under what circumstances, vary. As a result, the United States and Russia still face the quandary posed by Secretary Kissinger of making connections among policy goals, a declared strategy of deterrence, and the possession and potential employment of nuclear weapons in a way that is based on an understandable logic and conveys a credible argument to their current and possible future adversaries.[2]

The relationship between the United States and Russia plays an important role in how these strategies are developed as both sides contemplate their interests and efforts, the costs of their nuclear forces, the possibilities of arms control, and their desires for the future. While other issues and other countries affect both countries' nuclear thinking, as in the Cold War, the status of these two states as the possessors of the vast majority of the world's nuclear weapons creates a context in which day-to-day deterrence of unprovoked attack continues to play a role, even as both sides recognize that such an attack is improbable and increasingly unlikely. Also as in the Cold War, Europe continues to be the key focus of possible contention between these powers. This focus on "Europe" holds beyond the continent's borders (which, indeed, extend well into Russia)—for instance, to Georgia, since one basis of

---

[1]   Henry Kissinger, *Diplomacy*, New York: Simon and Schuster, p. 608.

[2]   Recent commission reports are clear in their belief that nuclear weapons remain useful tools for deterrence. See Office of the Secretary of Defense, *Report of the Secretary of Defense Task Force on DoD Nuclear Weapons Management: Phase II—Review of the DoD Nuclear Mission*, Washington, D.C., December 2008.

contention there is the shape and structure of Georgia's relationship to Europe. Concerns regarding NATO and U.S. relationships with and actions in the Central Asian states also play a role, although the nuclear component has been less evident.

Between the years 2000 and 2009, we saw a new development: Russia's assertion of particular interests within a deterrent framework it sought to establish with respect to the North Atlantic Treaty Organization (NATO) countries and particularly the United States. This effort included explicit recognition of the profound differences in the relative balance of conventional and nuclear military power and the mechanisms of modern war. In many ways, this effort reflected a revival of strategy and the reassertion of the deterrent value of nuclear weapons under conditions of conventional inferiority and for less than absolutely vital issues. As of February 2010, however, Russia appears to have reversed its stated policies on these issues, replacing a doctrine that advanced a calculated ambivalence about the possible use of nuclear weapons to secure Russian interests with a doctrine that is apparently more circumscribed regarding the circumstances under which nuclear use could be contemplated.

The monograph is organized as follows: Chapter Two describes the past elements of the deterrent framework (interests, military doctrine, force development, exercises, and endorsement by political and military authorities) and then describes how these have evolved in Russia since the end of the Cold War. Chapter Three uses the same elements in this deterrent framework to examine the evolution of Russia's deterrent framework with respect to the United States and the extent to which nuclear weapons figure in this framework. Chapter Four draws inferences with respect to an emergent Russian deterrent framework in Europe and elsewhere and seeks to define the limits of what can be surmised. Chapter Five raises the implications for the United States in terms of the issues that arise in defining its own deterrent framework, the potential role of arms control in supporting such a framework and in enhancing stability, and the implications for U.S. military planning and forces, and specifically for the Air Force.

CHAPTER TWO

Elements of a Deterrent Framework

During the Cold War, the Soviet Union and the United States established a deterrent framework that served to protect their vital, clearly stated interests and that involved the deployment of large numbers of conventional and nuclear weapons. Through presidential statements, formal alliance, and military deployments, the United States and the Soviet Union extended deterrence to include their NATO and Eastern European allies, respectively. Military doctrine was written and exercises undertaken to demonstrate the capacity of the weapon systems. We describe these claims and demonstrations of the willingness to defend them as elements of a deterrent framework.

The inter-German border as the boundary between the two systems—and the absolute authority of one system or the other depending on the side of that border—was the most long-lasting feature of the claims by both sides. The ability and willingness of each side to defend its claims with force, including nuclear weapons—and the unsatisfactory end-state of any such conflict no matter how the conflict initiated—was the central story of the Cold War as a study in deterrence.

Looking back, the deterrent framework had the following elements:[1]

- authoritative statement of claimed interests
- military doctrine and practice

---

[1] This monograph will not rehash the theoretical development of deterrence theory as played out by many distinguished political scientists. It will try to conform to the post–

- force development and posture
- major exercises and scenarios.

The first and most important element in the deterrent framework was a statement of the interests claimed, i.e., the interests that the adversary is deterred from infringing upon. The statement of interest was necessarily presented in understandable ways. The deployment of military forces reinforced the statement of interests. Following on was the authoritative propagation of thought and doctrine, the development and deployment of weapon systems, and the exercise of these systems, which indicated each country's beliefs about the likelihood of various conflicts and their intent in using military forces.

Today, the United States and Russia, which has inherited the nuclear arsenal of the USSR, are not enemies. Their interests converge in some areas but diverge in others. The two countries maintain global conventional and nuclear forces while at the same time seeking to negotiate reductions in strategic nuclear forces. What have these changes meant for the elements in Russia's deterrent framework?

First of all, the death of the Soviet Union as an ideological enterprise has removed political objectives based on ideology. The onus is on the Russian government to make its claims of interests through the mechanisms of a Russian state.

The doctrinal and equipment basis of the Russian armed forces are clearly a mixture of legacy and new products. Doctrine and military theory were influential components of how the Soviet military-political elite conceived their roles and how Western analysts examined Soviet intentions. The current Russian military elite continue to regard doctrine and theory as an important component of their approach to governing under the new order. To be useful, military doctrine and practice should, in the Russian view, provide the ability to deal with the types of conflicts that are implicitly or explicitly envisaged by the interests claimed in policy pronouncements. Moreover, there should be

---

Cold War cautions of Lawrence Freedman in trying to be clear about what actions are to be controlled (see Lawrence Freedman, *Deterrence*, Cambridge, UK: Polity Press, 2004). The principal arguments and theories of the Cold War period are summarized in Lawrence Freedman, *The Evolution of Nuclear Strategy*, 3rd ed., New York: Palgrave Macmillan, 2003.

visible agreement that military doctrine is not actually in conflict with pronounced government policies.

Over the nearly two decades since the end of the Soviet Union, the difficulties of forging a new civil-military relationship have frequently flared into public disputes among individuals personifying particular policy positions. These disputes are more than personality clashes; the rise and fall of individuals at the civil-military boundary provide indications of whether the translation of policy to practice across that boundary is working smoothly.

In Russian military doctrine and practice (as in that of other countries), there is a progression from the somewhat vague and sweeping public statements at the highest military-political levels to formulations of ever more detail and technical content, published as doctrines and strategic statements or presented as papers or speeches by lower-level officials, as the subject matter comes closer and closer to real military contingency or war plans, which, of course, remain classified. Parallel to the official doctrine and planning process is the military-scientific exposition and research that supports military education and information-sharing. Military and military-scientific officials in staff and educational organizations address the particular problems and solutions posed by the current and future situations and capabilities of potential adversaries. These efforts are collected in publications of varying authority that address problems in theoretical and (sometimes) great technical depth based on in-depth knowledge of the Russian military. In addition, serving military personnel, as well as their retired colleagues and civilian experts of varying degrees of influence, publish in commercially available journals and newspapers with a military or security focus. The authority of these publications can be gauged by a combination of the authority of the sponsoring institutions of the journal and, more importantly, that of the authors. The relevance of particular publications is also affected by the time frame in which they couch their results: obviously, the closer to the present the more relevant. Even so, starting with theoretical formulations in military-technical journals to reach conclusions about actual security planning at high military-political levels is a complicated process with many inherent uncertainties, far more so now than in the Soviet era.

Russia inherited many of the ongoing research and development programs of the old Soviet Union. In the past, the steady progression of prototype programs and their tests and trials was one of the most carefully followed indicators of Soviet military intentions. Many of the test programs—particularly missile systems—were amenable to analysis using the national technical means permitted and protected under arms control treaties. Moreover, the accumulation of experience with previous system introductions gave foreign analysts confidence that systems reaching particular milestones would appear within the operational force at predictable times.

While the simple continuance of such programs in some stage of slow-motion development may be an indication that Russia has the same intent that set the development in motion, it may also indicate bureaucratic inertia in the development community. To ascribe realized intent to current programs, it is necessary to look for corroboration in force structure and the status of actual units in the presence of so many half-active remnants of old programs.

The large military exercise as a military rehearsal and a political gesture is a unique inheritance from the Cold War confrontation in Europe. Both the East and the West annually conducted very large exercises involving hundreds of thousands of service members and thousands of aircraft and vehicles exercising portions of real war plans. The scenario time associated with such exercises was always the present or the very near future, and the scenarios were always based on existing forces and existing capabilities. Each country devoted great effort not only to conducting its own exercises but also to collecting real-time data on and subsequent in-depth analysis of the other side's exercises. As the Cold War settled into a stable form, the large autumn exercises gradually evolved toward ritualized displays of military prowess and capability on the part of the militaries, sustained commitment on the part of the political leaderships, and understanding on the part of the intelligence services. Familiarity with the other side's operating procedures and the somewhat convoluted confidence that "we know what they are doing and they know that we know" was a possibly stabilizing and certainly comforting factor in the relations between the two sides. With the benefit of hindsight, however, we realize that this comfort may have been a false comfort, for it is possible that the Soviets had a genuine war scare during the 1983 NATO exercise *Able Archer* and that Western intelligence was largely oblivious to this fear.[2] If this is true, or even possible, it provides a sobering lesson and underscores the importance of caution.

During the Soviet era, when the subordination of the Soviet military to the Politburo was largely unquestioned by Western analysts, anything carried out by the military could be assumed to precisely reflect the wishes of the political authorities. Today, given that Russia has been through a wrenching period of change and that the elements of policy, military forces, and exercises may sometimes be out of step, an additional element in a future deterrent framework will be needed: the endorsement by the highest political authorities of military doctrines, major exercises, and their scenarios. We feel that such endorsement clearly indicates that these reflect Russian policy and doctrine as the Russian government wishes it to be perceived, whereas the absence of such endorsement, or other disconnects between the various components of the framework, may indicate disagreement within the Russian government, lack of clarity in policy formulation, intentional obfuscation (whether for a domestic or foreign audience), or some combination of these.

---

[2]   This possibility was a grave concern to Robert Gates both in his then role at the Central Intelligence Agency and in his subsequent positions. See Robert M. Gates, *From the Shadows: The Ultimate Insider's Story of Five Presidents and How They Won the Cold War*, New York: Simon & Schuster, 1996, pp. 270–274. A contemporaneous Special National Intelligence Estimate responding to Gates's concerns has been declassified and posted at the Central Intelligence Agency's Freedom of Information Act Search page (Central Intelligence Agency, *Implications of Recent Soviet Military-Political Activities*, SNIE 11-10-84, May 11, 1984). The author of the SNIE reflects on its preparation and its judgments in Fritz W. Ermarth, "Observations on the 'War Scare' of 1983 from an Intelligence Perch," Parallel History Project on NATO and the Warsaw Pact, Stasi Intelligence on NATO, edited by Bernd Schaefer and Christian Nuenlist, November 6, 2003. The memory of the incident on the part of intelligence consumers was much more dramatic. See the treatment of this incident in the context of the current state of history on the end of the Cold War in Jeremy Suri, "Explaining the End of the Cold War: A New Historical Consensus," *Journal of Cold War Studies*, Vol. 4, No. 4, Fall 2002, pp. 60–92.

CHAPTER THREE

Russia's Claimed Interests and Military Planning in Europe

This chapter uses the elements in the past deterrent framework plus the element of endorsement by political authorities to examine why and how the Russians may be working to set up a deterrent framework with respect to the United States and the extent to which nuclear weapons figure in this framework. See Table 3.1 for a description of the framework. In developing and presenting this framework, we note

Table 3.1
Deterrent Framework Applied to Russian Military-Political Claims in Europe

Element of Framework	Description
Authoritative statement of claimed interests	Authoritative statement by the highest government authorities of the country's interests and purpose and how deployments of military forces reinforce these interests.
Military doctrine and practice	Authoritative propagation of thought and doctrine through formal doctrinal publications and their reflection in research journals. Individual military personnel action (selection, promotion, or demotion) on the basis of known espousal of particular policy or doctrinal views.
Force development and posture	Development, serial production, and acquisition of weapon systems; organization and equipment of military forces. Creation of forces and their placement.
Major exercises and scenarios	Major field exercises showing plans and intent. Scenarios showing beliefs about the likelihood of various conflicts—particularly important when there are public explanations of scenario features and the connections to Russian actions.
Endorsement of doctrine, forces, and exercises by political authorities	Reaffirmation of the intent, military leadership, and performance demonstrated in published doctrine and major exercises.

the importance of remaining sensitive to any presumptions and biases inherited by the analyst from the old way of doing things.

Statement of Claimed Interests

During the Cold War, the Soviet Union asserted its interests in Europe through the Warsaw Pact (formally, The Treaty of Friendship, Cooperation, and Mutual Assistance) that promised the same securities to its signatories as the North Atlantic Treaty and imposed Soviet leadership on the member militaries. With the dissolution of the Warsaw Pact, the eastern European countries that were not Soviet republics were left politically unconnected to the Russian successor state and, indeed, except for Poland, geographically separated from Russia. Russia itself went through a period of political uncertainty and internal weakness that is now being reversed as it moves to reassert its great-power status.[1]

The relationship of Russia to the other Soviet successor states has changed over time as the Soviet Union devolved into the Commonwealth of Independent States (CIS). The CIS is perhaps most visibly extant today in its Collective Security Treaty Organization, which was created by the Tashkent Treaty signed in 2002 by Armenia, Belarus, Kazakhstan, Kyrgyzstan, Russia, and Tajikistan and in 2006 by Uzbekistan. The Tashkent Treaty binds the states to regard aggression against one as aggression against all and further obliges them not to join other military alliances. There is a more extensive agreement with Belarus, described as political union, that has most recently manifested itself militarily as a regional integrated air defense network to be placed under a single Belarusian or Russian commander (apparently not yet named). In addition, Russia has now signed bilateral mutual assistance agreements with the Abkhazian and South Ossetian entities that have broken away from Georgia.

---

[1]   The broader resurgence of Russia and its reassertion of great-power interests is covered in Jeffrey Mankoff, *Russian Foreign Policy: The Return of Great Power Politics,* Lanham, Md.: Rowman & Littlefield, 2009.

Beyond the formal treaties, the new Russian statement of claimed interests is perhaps best captured by a television interview of President Dmitry Medvedev conducted in August 2008 shortly after the Georgian war. In the interview, Medvedev articulated five principles as the foundation of Russian foreign policy. These principles have come to be called the "Medvedev Doctrine." The last two principles claim certain interests beyond Russia's borders:

> Fourth, protecting the lives and dignity of our citizens, wherever they may be, is an unquestionable priority for our country. Our foreign policy decisions will be based on this need. We will also protect the interests of our business community abroad. It should be clear to all that we will respond to any aggressive acts committed against us.

> Finally, fifth, as is the case of other countries, there are regions in which Russia has privileged interests. These regions are home to countries with which we share special historical relations and are bound together as friends and good neighbours. These are the principles I will follow in carrying out our foreign policy.[2]

This carefully scripted portion of the interview was not just carried by Russian television stations but appears on the web page of the Russian president, both in Russian and in an English-language version.[3]

---

[2]   Principles 1–3 are as follows:

> First, Russia recognises the primacy of the fundamental principles of international law, which define the relations between civilised peoples. We will build our relations with other countries within the framework of these principles and this concept of international law. Second, the world should be multi-polar. A single-pole world is unacceptable. Domination is something we cannot allow. We cannot accept a world order in which one country makes all the decisions, even as serious and influential a country as the United States of America. Such a world is unstable and threatened by conflict. Third, Russia does not want confrontation with any other country. Russia has no intention of isolating itself. We will develop friendly relations with Europe, the United States, and other countries, as much as is possible. (Dmitry Medvedev, "Interview given by Dmitry Medvedev to Television Channels Channel One, Rossia, NTV," August 31, 2008)

[3]   President of Russia, website, 2011. Given the somewhat hit-or-miss quality of current American attention to Russia, it is perhaps best that the Russian government paid careful

The Medvedev Doctrine gives fuller expression to behaviors exemplified by the long-standing willingness of the Russians to retain troops described as peacekeepers in the de facto independent Trans-Dniester that has broken away from the Republic of Moldova, as well as the previous involvements in Abkhazia and South Ossetia. It is also consistent with an earlier presidential decree in 2007 to suspend observation of its treaty obligations under the Conventional Armed Forces in Europe (CFE) Treaty, which called for the removal of Russian forces from Moldova and Georgia. A subsequent explanatory document issued by the Russian president's office offered a number of reasons for the suspension. The first reason offered for suspension was the unacceptability of the NATO linkage of its own ratification of the treaty to the Russian presence in Georgia and Moldova. The Russian attachment to its claimed interests in these disputed territories and the provision of forces deployed to enforce those interests has been more important to Russia than any political costs incurred by abandoning the CFE Treaty.

Russian leaders have been clear with their statements about the importance of nuclear deterrence, but until the publication of its new military doctrine in February 2010 had not explicitly linked these to claimed interests or specifically identified what Russian nuclear forces are meant to deter. In March 2009, Medvedev told the Ministry of Defence staff that Russia's "nuclear deterrence [forces] must assuredly fulfill all tasks for securing Russia's military security."[4] This statement echoed one by his predecessor, Vladimir Putin, in 2006, who told participants in a meeting focused on the Russian nuclear weapon complex that "analysis of the current international situation and the prospects for its development force Russia to view nuclear deterrence as a basic element to guarantee and ensure its security."[5]

---

attention to making such statements available in approved versions.

[4]   Quoted in Press Center of Nuclear Energy and Industry, "Dmitry Medvedev Zaiavliaet o Neobkhodimosti Povisheniia Boegotovnosti Iadernikh Sil RF," citing *Interfax*, March 18, 2009.

[5]   Quoted in Sergei Belov, "Atom Sderzhivaniia," *Rossiiskaia Gazeta*, March 31, 2006. Author's translation of Putin statement.

Russian government statements on U.S. missile defense plans clarified the issue at least partially. Since the U.S. withdrew from the Anti-Ballistic Missile (ABM) Treaty and began substantial moves toward the creation of a national missile defense, Russian official statements have indicated a resilient belief that U.S. national missile defense is designed at least in part to counter Russian weapons and thus its deterrent capability. Russian officials at all levels have spoken clearly and consistently on this point.[6] It therefore follows that Russia continues to see its nuclear arsenal as, at least partially, existing to deter large-scale U.S. nuclear attack.

Military Doctrine and Practice

Doctrinal and Policy Writings

The Russian Ministry of Defence has adopted many of the communication features of the West and has its own website with both Russian- and English-language versions of key documents and current news items. The ministry publishes a "Defence Vision" (repeated under a separate heading as "Mission") that somewhat resembles an American national military strategy document condensed to a few pages and couched in more general terms.[7]

There is a certain similarity between the threats envisioned in American high-level documents and the existing Russian "Defence Vision." The Russian document creates a descriptive hierarchy of con-

---

[6]   In August 2008, Medvedev dismissed U.S. arguments that the systems that the U.S. then planned to deploy in Poland and the Czech Republic were not directed against Russia as "fairy tales." See Gordon Lubold, "Why U.S.-Poland Missile Deal Rouses Russian Bear," *Christian Science Monitor*, August 19, 2008. In July 2010, in an article on the new Strategic Arms Reduction Treaty (START), Russian Foreign Minister Sergei Lavrov indicated the need to monitor U.S. missile defense developments to ensure they do not threaten Russia's arsenal (Sergei Lavrov, "Novyi Dogovor o SNV v Matritse Global'noi Bezopasnosti," *Mezhdunarodnaia Zhizn'*, No. 7, July 2010, pp. 1–20). For more historical discussion of Russian missile defense views, see the missile defense discussions in Olga Oliker, Keith Crane, Lowell H. Schwartz, and Catherine Yusupov, *Russian Foreign Policy: Sources and Implications*, Santa Monica, Calif.: RAND Corporation, MG-768-AF, 2009.

[7]   Russian Ministry of Defence, "Mission," no date-b.

flict, relevant because it is drawn upon in other doctrinal and analytical work discussing nuclear weapons:

> The Armed Forces of the Russian Federation are maintained to fight the enemy in case of armed confrontations which can be classified into:
>
> ARMED CONFLICT. A type of political, ethnic, religious, territorial and other dispute resolution. It is a kind of an armed confrontation when neither of sides launches war activities while both sides normally seek their internal goals. An armed conflict may follow escalation of an armed incident, a border conflict, war actions or other local armed confrontation where armed military personnel take part.
>
> An armed conflict may be of an international (two or more states involved) or an internal (interstate confrontation) nature.
>
> LOCAL WAR. A war of limited political goals between two or more states. The warfare is normally conducted within the borders of opposing sides. The sides are primarily focused on their internal goals (territory, economy, politics or others).
>
> A local war is normally waged by task forces deployed in the zone of confrontation with possible increment through force projection, re-direction and partial strategic deployment.
>
> REGIONAL WAR. A war of two or more states (group of states) all located within a region when national armed forces or coalitions are employed. The warfare, thereat, is confined by one region, adjacent waters and airspace. All sides seek vital military and political goals. A regional war requires full deployment of armed forces and economy transformation, strengthening potentials of all sides. In cases when sides of confrontation (or their allies) possess nuclear weapons the regional war can potentially evolve into a nuclear warfare.
>
> LARGE-SCALE WAR. A war of coalitions or the most powerful nations of the world. It may be started as a result of a smaller

scale war escalation when more nations from different parts of the world join the confrontation. In a large-scale war the opposing sides seek uncompromising military and political goals. It requires the full mobilization of war reserves and high morale of troops.

The Russian Defence is planned with due regard to available reserves and capabilities of the national Armed Forces. To that end, the Armed Forces are required to be interoperable with other troops, must be able to counter a threat and defeat the enemy, be capable and active at both defence and offence under any circumstances of warfare or weapons used, including modern and future weapons and weapons of mass destruction.[8]

A somewhat more planning-oriented document that bridges the political-military boundary has been the National Security Concept. A version was issued in April 2000 early in Putin's first term as president. One of the most notable features of this document was a rather general treatment of threats but a blunt statement of the willingness to use nuclear weapons in dire situations:

> The Russian Federation considers the possibility of employing military force to ensure its national security based on the following principles:
>
> - use of all available forces and assets, including nuclear, in the event of need to repulse armed aggression, if all other measures of resolving the crisis situation have been exhausted and have proven ineffective;
>
> - use of military force inside the country is allowed in strict conformity with the Constitution of the Russian Federation and with federal laws in the event of emergence of a threat to citizens' lives and also of violent change to the constitutional system.[9]

---

[8]   Russian Ministry of Defence, no date-b.

[9]   Permanent Representation of the Russian Federation to the Council of Europe, "2000 Russian National Security Concept" (English version), 2000.

In May 2009, a new draft *National Security Strategy of the Russian Federation to 2020* was discussed at the Russian Security Council and approved at the presidential level. The document was more detailed than its antecedents and focused on the defining traits of an adversary that strongly resembled the United States.[10] This document enlarged the grounds for conflict to include struggles for resources on the Russian periphery. The detail made the precision-strike characteristics of the adversary more prominent as one of the advantages that must be overcome. Unlike its predecessor documents, however, it did not explicitly address the question of under what circumstances nuclear weapons might or might not be used. Rather, it underlined the need to maintain capable nuclear forces and to work toward the reduction and eventual abolition of nuclear weapons globally.[11]

Russia's new military doctrine, published in February 2010, clarified things considerably.[12] It replaced the last military doctrine, which dated from 2000 and indicated that Russia retains the right to use nuclear weapons in response to the use of weapons of mass destruction against it or its allies, as well as in response to conventional aggression in situations critical to Russian national security.[13] The new doctrine states that Russia sees its nuclear weapons as a tool of deterrence, necessary to prevent nuclear conflict or even conventional conflicts (large-scale or regional war). Moreover, it limits the possible use of nuclear weapons by Russia to circumstances in which nuclear and other types of weapons of mass destruction are used against Russia "and (or) its allies, and also in the event of aggression against the Russian Federation involving the use of conventional weapons when the very existence

---

[10] This candor comes in a Russian-language posting of the 2009 doctrine that has not been posted in English. See National Security Council of Russia, "Strategiia Natzional'noi Bezopasnosti Rossiiskoi Federatsii do 2020 Goda," Presidential Ukaz No. 537, May 12, 2009.

[11] National Security Council, 2009.

[12] National Security Council of Russia, "Voennaia Doktrina Rossiiskoi Federatsii," February 5, 2010.

[13] The 2000 doctrine is available in Russian on the website of Russia's National Security Council. See National Security Council of Russia, "Voennaia Doktrina Rossiiskoi Federatsii," Presidential Ukaz No. 706, April 21, 2000.

of the state is under threat." The 2010 doctrine also notes that the use of conventional force in a circumstance where the combatants possess nuclear weapons, and the existence of the state is threatened, could escalate into nuclear conflict.[14]

The new doctrine is supplemented by the classified *Foundations of Government Policy in the Area of Nuclear Deterrence Until 2020*, which was approved on the same day as the doctrine. We have no knowledge of its contents, but it reportedly lays out the criteria for nuclear weapon use in more detail.[15]

Thus, neither documents nor official statements leave any question that Russia sees its nuclear weapons as a necessary defense against other nuclear weapon states. In addition, as noted, Russia's declaratory policy, like that of the United States, does not preclude the use of nuclear forces, including first use (that is, against an enemy that has used conventional, chemical, or biological, but not nuclear, weapons).

Military-Scientific Literature

In contrast to the generalities of the Defence Vision, the military-scientific literature goes into more detail, in terms of both particular adversaries and proposed actions to deal with them. Specifically, this literature advances a view of the United States, and its nuclear forces, as a prospective threat in a number of contexts.

U.S. Nuclear Threat. Russian writing on nuclear strategic topics in prominent military- and security-focused journals and newspapers, as well as statements in such journals by military officers and government officials, indicate that many Russian analysts, including military analysts, believe that the United States actively seeks nuclear superiority (i.e., the ability to launch a debilitating first strike) to ensure its ability to influence Russia's policies and actions. Cited in support of this hypothesis are numerous Bush-era statements by U.S. officials and in U.S. documents regarding preventive war and the need to maintain U.S. military supremacy. Further support is seen in consistent U.S.

---

[14] National Security Council of Russia, 2010.

[15] "Rossiiskoe Iadernoe Oruzhie: Kriterii Primeneniia," *Natsional'naia Oborona*, No. 2, February 2010.

efforts to influence Russian policy throughout Russia's modern (post-Soviet) history.[16]

Furthermore, Russian officials and analysts assume that their country remains a focus of U.S. nuclear planning and scenarios, and cite public statements about Russia as a potential adversary and a focus of U.S. planning by U.S. officials to support this. Russian analysts who speak of the U.S. threat in this context often present an image of a hostile and aggressive United States taking consistent action to threaten and provoke Russia through submarine patrols, intercepts of Russian bomber flights, and NATO enlargement.[17]

Although some couch concerns about the United States in the language of capabilities, rather than intentions, many Russian analysts also describe U.S. policy as inherently aggressive in nature, predicated on the use of force to attain policy goals, and as misaligned with Rus-

---

[16]   For discussions of these issues and related ones, see Richard Weitz, *Russian-American Security Cooperation After St. Petersburg: Challenges and Opportunities*, Carlisle, Pa.: Strategic Studies Institute, 2007; Andrei Kokoshin, "'Assimmetrichnyi Otvet' Vs. 'Strategicheskoi Oboronnoi Initsiativy,'" *Mezhdunarodnaia Zhizn'*, No. 7, August 2007, pp. 29–42; A. IU. Maruev, "Voennye Aspekty Formirovaniia Geopoliticheskikh Interesov I Geostrategii Rosii," *Voennaia Mysl*, No. 1, January 2009, pp. 2–8; Vladimir Lutovinov, "Sistema Voennykh Ugroz Bezopasnosti Rossii: Voenno-Politicheskii Analiz," *Voennye Znaniia*, No. 1, January 2009, pp. 2–4; Vladlen Malyshev and E'duard Bogatyriev, "Voennye Ugrozy I Ikh Vliianie na Planirovanie Mereopriiatii Grazhdanskoi Oborony," *Voennye Znaniia*, No. 5, May 2009, pp. 35–37; Igor' Korotchenko, "Sokhranit' Potentsial Otvetnogo Udara," *Voenno-Promyshlennyi Kur'er,* No. 20, May 27, 2009, p. 1; Kirill Troitskii, "Vo Imia 'Global'nogo Poriadka?'" *Voenno-Promyshlennyi Kur'er*, No. 20, May 27, 2009, p. 10; Vadim Mamlyga, "Ucheniia V Gruzii: Chto Za Factom? Igra Na Vyzhivanie," *Flag Rodiny*, No. 94 June 2, 2009, p. 5; M. A. Gareev, "Problemy Strategicheskogo Sderzhivaniia v Sovermennykh Usloviiakh," *Voennaia Mysl*, No. 4, April 2009 pp. 2–9; E. S. Sirotinin, "Sderzhivanie Agressii v Kontekste Novoi Voennoi Doktriny Rossiiskoi Federatsii," *Voennaia Mysl*, No. 5, May 2010, pp. 3–9. Russian critiques of these views can be found in, among others, Iurii Kirshin, "Osnovopolagaiushchie Printsipy Zashchity Strany," *Nezavisimoe Voennoe Obozrenie*, No. 13, April 10, 2009, p. 12; Vadim Solov'ev, "Strategiia—Novaia, Podkhody—Konservativnye," *Nezavisimoe Voennoe Obozrenie*, No. 17, May 22, 2009; and Aleksandr Khramchikhin, "Smes' Iz Kompleksov, Samoobmana I Obmana," *Nezavisimoe Voennoe Obozrenie*, No. 18, May 29, 2009a, p. 1.

[17]   Lutovinov, 2009; Malyshev and Bogatyriev, 2009; Korotchenko, 2009; Troitskii, 2009. See also Vladimir Kozin, "IAdernye Dilemmy," *Krasnaia Zvezda*, No. 90, May 22, 2009, p. 3.

sian goals and policies in key areas.[18] In a critique of Washington's 2010 *Nuclear Posture Review Report,* a Russian Foreign Ministry official argues that this document permits the United States to carry out a nuclear strike even when the United States has not been attacked (in contrast to the Russian doctrine, which predicates nuclear use on attack).[19]

Russian analysts are consistent, therefore, in viewing Russia's nuclear arsenal as existing to deter the United States on a day-to-day basis from the unlikely actuality of a debilitating first strike and from the coercion the capacity to launch such an attack allows Washington to exercise. The nuclear deterrent protects Russia from coercion and allows it to advance its interests and have them respected by other states.[20] Russia must therefore maintain an arsenal of a size roughly equal to that of the United States and substantially larger than that of any other nuclear powers. It also means that Russia must have a second-strike capability against U.S. forces, to constrain the United States from fielding a force that can launch that debilitating first strike. U.S. missile defense plans are therefore seen as a means to overcome Russia's second-strike capability, and thus as harmful to overall stability in the nuclear context.[21]

Some Russian analysts worry that the United States is already able to disable Russia's second-strike capability. Here, the vision of the American high-technology adversary and the perfection of the reconnaissance-strike complex method of war combine with concerns about the U.S. desire for nuclear preeminence into a fear that, should war be likely, the United States would launch a first strike against Russia,

---

[18] M. A. Gareev and I. V. Erokhin, "Kakie Vooruzhennye Sily Nuzhny Rossii," *Voennaia Mysl,* No. 4, April 2009, pp. 61–65; A. A. Protasov, S. V. Kreidin, and S. IU. Egorov, "Sistemy Upravleniia Voiskami (Silami) Kak Instrument Strategicheskogo Sderzhivaniia," *Voennaia Mysl,* No. 7, July 2009, pp. 8–11.

[19] Vladimir Kozin, "Novaia IAdernaia Doktrina SSHA: Anakhronism Sokhraniaetsia," *Natsional'naia Oborona,* No. 4, April 2010.

[20] Lutovinov, 2009; Leonid Grigor'evich Ivashov, "Podozritel'naia Speshka v Sokrashchenii IAdernikh Vooruzhenii," *Nezavisimaia Gazeta,* July 6, 2009b.

[21] Kokoshin, 2007; Kozin, 2010; Ivashov, 2009b; Lavrov, 2010.

targeting its strategic nuclear forces, so as to ensure that Russia cannot retaliate.[22] Some of this analysis is conducted within the context of a "bolt-out-of-the-blue," in which the United States not only launches a first-strike but does so from a posture in which there has been no prior crisis leading to heightened alert on the part of the Russian defense.

Concerns that the United States has a first-strike advantage are not new, but they began receiving particular attention in 2006, following the publication in the United States of two articles by Keir Leiber and Daryl Press that argued that the combination of U.S. missile defenses and its nuclear and conventional capabilities could result in an effective debilitating first strike against Russia's arsenal.[23] When the Lieber and Press articles first appeared, their conclusions were hotly debated in Russia, and many analysts insisted that the articles were somehow authorized by the U.S. government.[24] At the same time, Russian- and U.S.-based specialists argued then, and continue to argue now, that Russia retains a capable second-strike capability and can overcome U.S. missile defenses (including planned missile defenses) with current and developing technology.[25] Official Russian opinion is

---

[22]   Sirotinin, 2010.

[23]   Keir A. Lieber and Daryl G. Press, "The Rise of U.S. Nuclear Primacy," *Foreign Affairs*, Vol. 85, No. 2, March–April 2006b; Keir A. Lieber and Daryl G. Press, "The End of MAD: The Nuclear Dimension of U.S. Primacy," *International Security*, Vol. 30, No. 4, Spring 2006a, pp. 7–44.

[24]   Kokoshin calls them "trial balloons."

[25]   Alexei Arbatov and Vladimir Dvorkin, "Nuclear Deterrence: History, Current State, and Future Prospects," in Alexei Arbatov and Vladimir Dvorkin, eds., *Nuclear Weapons After the Cold War,* Carnegie Moscow Center, Moscow: R. Elinin Publishing House, 2008; Kokoshin; Paul Podvig, "Speaking of Nuclear Primacy," Russian Strategic Nuclear Forces website (russianforces.org), March 10, 2006a; Paul Podvig, "Russia Discusses Nuclear Weapons," Russian Strategic Nuclear Forces website (russianforces.org), March 31, 2006b; Paul Podvig, "Nuclear Primacy Again," Russian Strategic Nuclear Forces website (russianforces. org), August 22, 2006c; Igor' Korotchenko, "SNV, PRO i Budushchee Rosiiskikh Strategicheskikh IAdernykh Sil," *Natsional'naia Oborona*, No. 4, April 2010 (this is an interview with General Constructor of Moscow Institute of Thermotechnics [thermal engineering] Yurii Solomonov); Viktor Esin, "SShA: Kurs Na Global'nuyu PRO," *Voenno-Promyshlennyi Kur'er*, No. 33, August 31, 2010, p. 5.

with this group, although concerns that U.S. missile defense capabilities could develop so as to threaten the Russian deterrent remain.[26]

U.S. Strategic Conventional Military Threat. The Russian vision of America as a military adversary is dominated by U.S. precision-strike capabilities. Even before Operation Desert Storm (ODS) and the First Gulf War, the Soviets had begun to credit the Americans with work toward a "reconnaissance-strike complex" that pulled together multiple sensor assets with real-time control and rapid weapon delivery to targets throughout the depth of the theater of military operations. ODS showed both the possibilities and the limitations of this approach at the time under conditions of air supremacy. In the immediate aftermath of ODS, an influential commentator in *Aviation and Cosmonautics* could discount the extent of American success with aerial reconnaissance as "Its successes started in places where data was required on stationary targets and ended in places where immediate information was needed on mobile targets located deep in enemy territory."[27]

Since ODS, the Russians have watched American capabilities progress through additional investment, force modernization, and claims of a new American style of warfare. Although American air operations in Kosovo are now largely forgotten by the American military that carried them out, Russian memories of "contactless war" are both strong and pointed. First, American diplomacy disregarded Russian interests and representations in the run-up to the conflict and painfully underlined America's then-current valuation of Russia's powerlessness. In addition, American ability to quickly achieve air supremacy and wear away Serb forces without putting American or NATO ground forces at risk in the theater at all (hence "contactless war") telegraphed (whether intentionally or not) that Russia could be treated in the same way should the countries come to conflict in the future.

---

[26] Lavrov, 2010.

[27] V. Dubrov, "Aviation in Local Wars: In Search of New Tactics," *Aviatsiia i Kosmonautika*, October 1991, translated in JPRS-UAC-92-005, May 4, 1992, pp. 12–14. Russian contemporary lessons of ODS are discussed in James T. Quinlivan, "Soviet Air and Air Defense Forces and Their Successors, Lessons from the Gulf War," in Theodore W. Karasik, *Russia and Eurasia Armed Forces Review Annual, Volume 15—1991*, Gulf Breeze, Fl.: Academic International Press, 1999.

In the strategic nuclear context, this has led air defense specialist E. S. Sirotinin, for example, to argue that conventional war with the United States is impossible, because the United States would seek to eliminate Russian strategic nuclear retaliatory capability in any scenario, which in turn would lead to Russian nuclear use.[28] Russian Academy of Military Sciences President M. A. Gareev stops short of this formulation but indicates that continued deterrence of the United States will long be necessary because the two countries' interests are at odds.[29]

America's ability to weld information and strike assets is by itself the principal reason why Russian military thinkers came to the concept of employing nuclear weapons in theater settings.[30] Indeed, it appears that Russian analysts and officials have come to see U.S. strategic conventional superiority and reach (and formulations such as "prompt global strike") as dangerous. A number of arguments are made in this context. One is that the United States has a far lower threshold for strategic conventional use, and thus Russia is in more danger of attack with conventional weapons (to which it might have to respond with nuclear weapons). Another is that the United States or another adversary might use conventional strategic weapons to strike at Russian nuclear silos and other weapon facilities.[31] For example, a recent article

---

[28] Sirotinin, 2010.

[29] Gareev, 2009.

[30] This derives in large part from Major General Slipchenko's concepts of the successive generations of war and the American ability to wage "sixth-generation war" comprising employment of advanced conventional weapons, automated control systems, radio-electronic combat, precision strike, and weapons based on new physical principles. See Vladimir I. Slipchenko, "Russian Analysis of Warfare Leading to the Sixth Generation," *Field Artillery*, October 1993, pp. 38–41. This is analyzed at length in Jacob W. Kipp, "Russia's Nonstrategic Nuclear Weapons," *Military Review*, May–June 2001. See also Slipchenko's longer treatments of this issue in book form: Vladimir I. Slipchenko and M. A. Gareev, *Voina Budushchego: Shestoe Pokolenie*, Moscow: Mosckovskiy Obshchestvenniy Nauchniy Fond, 1999; and Vladimir I. Slipchenko, *Bezkontaktnye Voiny*, Moscow: Gran Press, 2001. See also Rose Gottemoeller, "Nuclear Necessity in Putin's Russia," *Arms Control Today*, April 2004.

[31] Viktor Ruchkin, "V Poiskakh Paradigmy Stabil'nosti," *Krasnaia Zvezda*, No. 68, April 16, 2009, p. 1; Evgenii Akhmerov, Oleg Bogdanov, and Marat Valeev, "Neobkhodimosti v Zenitnom Raketnom Prikrytii RVSN Net," *Vozdushno-Kosmicheskaia Oborona*, No. 3,

in the Russian journal *Vozdushno-Kosmicheskaia Oborona* (*Air-Space Defense*) evaluates the costs and benefits of anti-aircraft defenses of the strategic rocket forces. Its authors, air defense specialists, postulate how an attack might occur and what Russia's second-strike capability might be. They argue that, in attempting a debilitating strike, the United States, as the most capable prospective aggressor, might begin with a non-nuclear strike on Russian silo-based intercontinental ballistic missiles (ICBMs), combined with the destruction of the other two legs of Russia's triad, by means unspecified. This would be followed by an assessment of damage and only then a nuclear strike. If this were the case, they posit, Russia would likely retain the capability to launch a second strike. Even if the first strike is nuclear, they note, the enemy would still face the problem of attacking mobile missiles.[32]

Defending Against Strategic Threats: Launch on Warning? The authors of the *Vozdushno-Kosmicheskaia Oborona* (*Air-Space Defense*) piece cited above conclude that, given the possibility of a conventional or nuclear strike against Russia's strategic nuclear forces, Russia is better off investing in early warning capability than anti-aircraft defenses.[33] Early warning is also the theme of another paper in the same journal, this one by three space warfare specialists. They argue that improved early warning will enable Russia to more effectively launch its weapons on warning of a U.S. attack, explicitly described as a better option than a responsive second strike.[34] Indeed, early warning has become a theme in recent Russian writing on deterrence, with a number of articles arguing that improvements to the system are crucial.[35] These argu-

---

2009, pp. 32–37; Sirotinin, 2010; "Rossiiskoe Iadernoe Oruzhie: Kriterii Primeneniia," 2010.

[32] Akhmerov, Bogdanov, and Valeev, 2009.

[33] Akhmerov, Bogdanov, and Valeev, 2009.

[34] Igor Morozov, Sergei Baushev, and Oleg Kaminskii, "Kosmos i Kharakter Sovremennykh Voennykh Deistvii," *Vozdushno-kosmicheskaia Oborona*, No. 4, 2009, pp. 48–56.

[35] Akhmerov, Bogdanov, and Valeev, 2009; Morozov, Baushev, and Kaminskii, 2009; Sirotinin, 2010; Sergei Sukhanov, "VKO—Eto Zadacha, a Ne Sistema," *Vozdushno-Kosmicheskaia Oborona*, No. 2, 2010, pp. 6–12; Sergei Nesterov and Sergei Volkov, "Eshche Raz o Sisteme VKO," *Vozdushno-Kosmicheskaia Oborona*, No. 4, 2010, pp. 6–13; Arkadii Borzov,

ments, of course, imply that the system as it stands today is insufficient (a postulate supported by the facts, as we will discuss later). Similarly, discussions of the need for better command and control systems for nuclear and strategic forces, and for the need for more thoughtful and robust nuclear planning, lest Russia be unable to sustainably deter a U.S. or other attack, imply deficiencies in these areas, as well.[36]

Changing the alert condition of the strategic forces to respond to threat conditions and to signal within crisis have both negative and positive aspects. Indeed, Gareev argues that mobilization of nuclear forces can be a form of and step in deterrence in and of itself.[37] Within the existing pattern of strategic force operations, such mobilization could include movement of mobile ICBMs from garrison location, sending nuclear ballistic missile submarine (SSBNs) to sea, and visibly arming bomber aircraft with full cruise missile payloads.

It is also worth noting in this context what may be a casual translation in a recent article by some of the biggest names in arms control in Russia: Sergei Rogov, Pavel Zolatarev, Viktor Esin, and Valerii Iarynich. In a co-authored piece, they define "otvetno-vstrechniy udar," which literally translates as "response-to-meet strike," as "launch on warning" and allow for no possibility to "launch under attack" (that is, when attack has been definitively ascertained).[38] If Russia does not trust its early warning systems to enable it to know when an attack is

---

"VKO: Pora Prekratit' Terminologicheskie Diskussii," *Vozdushno-Kosmicheskaia Oborona*, No. 4, 2010, pp. 14–25.

[36] On command and control, see Andrei Kokoshin, *Strategicheskoe Upravlenie: Teoria, Istoricheskiy Opyt, Sravnitel'ny Analiz, Zadachi Dlia Rossii*, Moscow: MGIMO Press, ROSSPEN Publishers, 2003; and Protasov, Kreidin, and Egorov, 2009, pp. 8–11. On planning, see the excellent V. V. Matvichuk and A. L. Khriapkin, "Sistema Strategicheskogo Sderzhivaniia v Novykh Usloviiakh," *Voennaia Mysl*, No. 1, January 2010, pp. 11–16. For more general concerns that Russia's posture is insufficient to deter the United States, see also Maruev, 2009; I. V. Erokhin, "Kakie Vooruzhennye Sily Nuzhny Rossii," *Voennaia Mysl*, No. 4, April 2009, pp. 61–65; and Gareev, 2009.

[37] Gareev, 2009.

[38] Sergei Rogov, Pavel Zolatarev, Viktor Esin, and Valerii Iarynich, "Sud'ba Strategicheskikh Vooruzhenii Posle Pragi, *Nezavisimoe Voennoe Obozrenie*, No. 32, August 27, 2010, p. 1.

underway, launch on warning—which could mean launch on erroneous warning—indeed becomes more likely.

Other Threats That Could Lead to a Nuclear Response. The concept that a large-scale U.S. attack, nuclear or conventional, on strategic nuclear forces would require a nuclear response on the part of Russia aligns with the new nuclear doctrine and its focus on nuclear use in cases where foreign attack threatens the existence of the state.

However, in the military-scientific literature that discusses possible scenarios for nuclear use, a large-scale disarming nuclear attack is not the only possibility. Another family of scenarios postulated by Russian analysts for nuclear use exists at a lower level of conflict. The same vision of American high-technology and precision capabilities forms the basis of writings on the potential escalation of regional and local conflict: Russia may be drawn in through an international peacekeeping mission that escalates into a major conflict, creating a premise for general war, and thus potential for nuclear weapon use or threat of use.[39] The United States is not the only possible threat in this context. China is discussed as a possible aggressor by some analysts, and dismissed as such by others.[40] Some authors go so far as to list countries deemed capable of large-scale "armed aggression" against Russia and its forces. These of course include the United States, its NATO allies, and China. In some conceptions, they also include other countries or groups thereof. One author describes what he terms (without naming specific examples) "developing countries possessing mass armies"

---

[39] Lutovinov, 2009; Malyshev and Bogatyriev, 2009.

[40] Aleksandr Khramchikhin is particularly vocal about the China threat. See, for example, Aleksandr Khramchikhin, "Starye Osnovy Novoi Doktriny," *Voenno-Promyshlennyi Kur'er*, No. 6, February 17, 2010a, p. 5; Aleksandr Khramchikhin, "Illiuziia IAdernogo Sderzhivaniia," *Voenno-Promyshlennyi Kur'er*, No. 11, March 24, 2010b, p. 1; and Aleksandr Khramchikhin, "Neadekvatnyi Vostok," *Nezavisimoe Voennoe Obozrenie*, No. 27, July 23, 2010c, p. 1. Maruev (2009) may also allude to China in a discussion of countries that seek Russian territory, and Gareev (2009) indicates that China is not a true ally of Russia. For a response to China threat arguments, particularly Khramchikhin's, see Sergei Kazennov and Vladimir Kumachev, "Ne Nado Absoliutizirovat' 'Ugrozu S Vostoka," *Nezavisimoe Voennoe Obozrenie*," No. 30, August 13, 2010, p. 12. Sirotinin (2010) argues that China might try to attack Russian nuclear capabilities in a conflict, but would fail to eliminate Russian capacity to respond.

(defined as those that comprise 5 to 10 percent of their populations). This analyst also includes states possessing or developing ballistic missile technology and chemical weapons as potential threats.[41]

In the context of possible escalation involving U.S. forces specifically, however, the thinking has been long-term. The appreciation that conflict with American or NATO forces could put conventional Russian ground forces at risk, with little prospect that the depleted Russian air and air defense forces could offer any protracted defense, motivated a number of selective escalatory mechanisms. The key concept offered by the Russian military-theoretical community at the end of the last decade was the "de-escalation of military actions." Put concisely, the concept is that nuclear weapon use in theater might be done not just for military effect but also as a means to induce an adversary to de-escalate the conflict. The paper that introduced the idea to the military-theoretical community appeared in *Voyennaya Mysl*, the journal of the Russian General Staff, in 1999, authored by Major General Levshin and Colonels Nedelin and Sosnovsky. This short paper put forward a set of assertions and ideas that capture both a Russian appreciation of their conventional disadvantage and the utility of nuclear weapons.[42]

The particular utility of the Levshin et al. paper is that it put forward assertions and questions very early in the Russian process of rethinking the role of nuclear weapons in theater, well before official sensitivities could constrain thinking or conceal sensitive decisions. The paper does not offer answers to all of its questions or necessary decisions, but its recognition of the existence of the question is itself important, particularly as scenarios of conflict escalation continue to be postulated, as noted above. The clarity of the key elements exam-

---

[41]   Lutovinov, 2009. A similar argument is included in Leonid Ivashov, "Politicheskaya Tsena Iadernoi' Bomby, *Nezavisimoe Voennoe Obozrenie*, No. 19, June 5, 2009a, p. 1.

[42]   V. I. Levshin, A. V. Nedelin, and M. E. Sosnovsky, "O Primenenii IAdernogo Oruzhiia Dlia Deeskalatsii Voennykh Deistvii, [On Employing Nuclear Weapons to De-Escalate Military Operations]," *Voyennaya Mysl [Journal of Military Thought: A Russian Journal of Military Theory and Strategy]*, May–June 1999, pp. 34–37. The original paper was identified as a critical new element in the Russian approach to war. See the seminal paper by Jacob W. Kipp (2001). Also David S. Yost, "Russia's Non-Strategic Nuclear Forces." *International Affairs*, Vol. 77, No. 3, *Changing Patterns of European Security and Defence*, July 2001, pp. 531–551.

ined in the Levshin et al. paper include the command level of decisions for weapon employment, the selection of targets, selection of weapon type, and the basic logic of how de-escalation is to follow from nuclear weapon use.

On the question of "Who controls?" Levshin, Nedelin, and Sosnovsky write, "The essential thing, however, will be who controls the asset: the Supreme Commander-in-Chief or the commander-in-chief of the armed forces in the theatre of operations," with "The initial employment is on the basis of a decision adopted by the Supreme Commander-in-Chief and only in accordance with a separate order (signal) issued by the Defense Minister."

On the choice of weapons, the Levshin paper emphasizes non-strategic nuclear weapons, primarily operational-tactical nuclear weapons. Non-strategic nuclear weapons include operational-strategic (long-range bombers and sea-based long-range cruise missiles carried by attack submarines) and operational-tactical and tactical (carrier aircraft of front and naval aviation, missile and artillery systems of land forces, missile and torpedo systems of naval general purpose forces, anti-aircraft missile systems, and nuclear mines of the engineer troops). Separately, Levshin and his co-authors make the point that "The most acceptable type of weapon for this kind of impact may be represented by sea-based long-range cruise missiles, which are launched from nuclear-powered attack submarines, this fact meaning that the strike will not involve strategic nuclear weapons."

On the topic of the escalatory ladder, Levshin and his co-authors suggest singling out the following stages of operational-tactical nuclear weapon (OTNW) employment: demonstration, intimidation-demonstration, intimidation, intimidation-retaliation. The authors provide particular examples of target sets corresponding to these descriptors. Table 3.2 shows the correspondence between these purposes and potential targets.

On the logic of de-escalation, the authors write, "A phased, intimidating employment of OTNW in combination with a demonstration of readiness to employ SNW [strategic nuclear weapons] may become the most powerful inducement for an aggressor to scale down military operations."

Table 3.2
Selected OTNW Employment Stages and Corresponding Target Set
Examples from the Levshin, Nedelin, and Sosnovsky Paper

Characterization	Target Set
Demonstration	Single demonstrative strike against desert or water areas or minor sparsely manned or entirely unmanned military facilities.
Intimidation-demonstration	Single nuclear strikes at transportation hubs or engineer installations, to localize area of military operations and reduce efficiency of invading troops at the operational or operational-tactical level without causing high losses.
Intimidation	Multiple strikes against the main force in a single operational sector to change balance of forces and/or eliminate an enemy breakthrough to the operational depth of defenses.
Intimidation-retaliation	Concentrated strikes at enemy theater of operation force groupings within the limits of one or several adjacent operational sectors if a defense operation takes an unfavorable turn. Objectives: to remove the threat of a rout of a friendly force, to resolutely change the balance of forces in an operational sector, to eliminate an enemy breakthrough of a defensive line held by an operational-strategic large unit.
Retaliation-intimidation	Massed strike against an aggressor's armed forces through a theater of operations, to rout it and achieve a radical change in the military situation in one's favor.
Retaliation	Delivery of a massed strike or strikes at the adversary within the limits of an entire theater of war (if necessary, involving military-economic targets of the aggressor) characterized by the maximum use of all forces and assets and coordination with strikes launched by the strategic nuclear forces, if these are going to be employed.

SOURCE: Levshin, Nedelin, and Sosnovsky, 1999.

Although the Levshin et al. article might appear dated, nonstrategic nuclear use continued to be raised both in the escalation scenarios cited above and in other contexts. In 2009, Vice Admiral Oleg Burtsev, Deputy Chief of the Russian Federation Navy Main Staff, talked of an increased role for "tactical" nuclear weapons.[43] At least one analyst has recently explicitly described tactical nuclear weapons as an important component of deterrence, including of the United States.[44] Other

---

[43] "RF Budet Uvelichivat' Rol' Takticheskogo Iadernogo Oruzhiia Na Mnogotselevykh APL," *Gazeta* (gzt.ru), March 23, 2009.

[44] Ivashov, 2009b.

authors argue for the importance of improving command and control systems for nonstrategic weapons (which these authors say have fallen by the wayside with the priority given to strategic forces).[45] As already noted, Sirotinin holds that any conflict with the United States would necessarily escalate to a nuclear conflict, though he envisions this happening rather quickly, rather than through an escalatory ladder.[46] Conversely, in a thoughtful take on deterrence today, two Russian strategic experts argue that while in peacetime the role of deterrence is to prevent war, in wartime it involves steps that can de-escalate aggression and end combat early on terms favorable to Russia and its allies and prevent nuclear war, suggesting the possibility of conventional escalation that does not lead to nuclear use.[47]

Prior to the publication of Russia's February 2010 doctrine, it appeared that this concept of nuclear use might just take hold. Statements by Russian Security Council Secretary Nicolai Patrushev to the newspaper *Izvestiia* in October 2009 referenced the hierarchy of wars laid out in the Defence Vision, indicated that the new doctrine would describe the conditions under which nuclear weapons could be used to counter conventional aggression, and indicated that this would include regional and local wars as well as large-scale war. Patrushev also noted that Russia would not exclude the possibility of a "preventive" nuclear strike.[48] Once the doctrine was published, however, Patrushev told the *Krasnaia Zvezda* newspaper that the new doctrine means that Russia's nuclear weapons are a tool of deterrence and that Russia would reserve the right to use them "in response to the use of nuclear or other weapons of mass destruction against the Russian Federation and its allies, and in the event of conventional aggression against Russia if there is a

---

[45] Protasov, Kreidin, and Egorov, 2009. For more on command and control, see Kokoshin, 2003.

[46] Sirotinin, 2010.

[47] Matvichuk and Khriapkin, 2010.

[48] Vladimir Mamontov, "Meniaetsia Rossiia, Meniaetsia i Ee Voennaia Doktrina," *Izvestiia*, October 14, 2009.

threat to the existence of the state itself, its territorial integrity, and its inviolability."[49]

Interpreting the New Doctrine. The seeming disconnect between Patrushev's statements in the fall and the actual doctrine (and his words subsequent to its publication) raises questions. Because we do not know what the classified *Foundations of Government Policy in the Area of Nuclear Deterrence Until 2020* specifies, we can only speculate as to the shape of doctrinal guidance for the future of Russia's nuclear planning. In an unsigned article in Igor' Korotchenko's journal, *Natsional'naia Oborona*, an effort is made to lay out possible criteria in line with the doctrine. The article notes that in the event of a missile launch against Russia, Russia could launch under attack or wait to respond. It postulates that a massive missile strike would surely result in retaliation against the United States and its nuclear-armed allies (the United Kingdom and France) but notes that a single missile might be cause for a hotline telephone call to Washington, and possibly a reciprocal response. It also lays out possible criteria for a nuclear response to conventional attack, namely if that attack involves:

- attacks on Russian political-administrative and economic centers, such as Moscow, St. Petersburg, Novosibirsk, Ekaterinburg, Vladivostok, and others
- attacks on military space systems or early warning system
- attacks on general staff command points
- attacks on the Strategic Rocket Forces (SRF)
- attacks on air bases hosting strategic aviation
- attacks on naval bases that host submarine-launched ballistic missiles (SLBMs)
- attacks on Russian SLBMs carrying out patrols
- attacks by enemy ground forces on Russian territory if Russian conventional forces cannot halt their progress.[50]

---

[49]   Quoted in Matvei Kozhukin, "Iadernoe Oruzhie—Faktor Sderzhivaniia," *Krasnaia Zvezda*, February 10, 2010.

[50]   "Rossiiskoe Iadernoe Oruzhie: Kriterii Primeneniia," 2010.

Interestingly, and somewhat disturbingly, this piece ends with the argument that, given U.S. strategic advantages over Russia, Russia must "intensify" efforts to develop a "dead hand" system that can carry out a second strike without human involvement, should the U.S. attack have destroyed Russian leadership.[51] Whatever the debates Russia has had, and may still be having, about escalation to nuclear use, the possibility of a debilitating U.S. attack remains at the forefront of strategic thinking in the military-scientific establishment.

Force Development and Posture

During the Cold War, the most serious indicator of Soviet intentions was the development and procurement of military systems that gave insight into the willingness and methods of using force. The number of Soviet tactical systems and their range of capabilities combined with the conscription of millions of men gave little doubt that the Soviets were capable of offensive war in Europe. Similarly, the regular modernization and introduction of nuclear systems that saw steady increases in numbers and performance, combined with the modernization of extensive air defenses and the only deployed ABM system (deployed around Moscow), demonstrated commitment that sought military and political advantages by preparing to fight—and perhaps win—a nuclear war.[52]

---

[51]   "Rossiiskoe Iadernoe Oruzhie: Kriterii Primeneniia," 2010.

[52]   In retrospect, the connection between this outcome and the underlying Soviet intent is becoming more complicated as historians gain access to contemporary archives and direct access to participants. For example, the Office of Net Assessment initiated one of the first such efforts in John G. Hines, Ellis M. Mishulovich, and John F. Shull, *Soviet Intentions 1965-1985, Volume I: An Analytical Comparison of U.S.-Soviet Assessments During the Cold War*, McLean, Va.: BDM Federal, Inc., September 1995. Drawing on interviews with participants, the authors see the military industrialists as having great influence in the introduction of new systems and their serial production. Subsequent research in the archives of that period has provided further evidence on the extent to which military expenditures drained the Soviet economy. A recent exposé is David E. Hoffman, *The Dead Hand: The Untold Story of the Cold War Arms Race and Its Dangerous Legacy*, New York: Doubleday, 2009.

With the demise of the Soviet Union, Russia inherited much of the Soviet military force structure and most of the ongoing weapon system development programs. At the same time, these assets lost much of their meaning as indicators of intentions because of the genuine confusion over whether their continued existence represented actual commitments, simple bureaucratic inertia, or even work programs for military or civilian workforces. Very few systems or deployments could be tied to particular new policies.

In the past decade, an effort has been made to reenergize the Russian military-industrial sector, but its capabilities have been sharply reduced. In this context, one could argue that Russia's force development is therefore more reflective of strategy than it may have been during the Cold War. However, no less plausible is the argument that fear of the sector's further weakening drives force development just as much as strategy does. Either way, current military forces and acquisition programs are necessarily lagged indicators reflecting decisions made in the past. Announced plans presumably reflect current intentions and decisions, but—much more than in the Cold War—announced plans in today's Russia have had a tendency to miss deadlines, fail critical milestones, and drift off into the next announced plan. Thus, it is critical that Russian statements of plans be understood as just that—and that analysts recognize that a variety of priorities and interests will be reflected both in those plans and in the degree of their implementation.

Strategic Nuclear ICBMs

Perhaps the clearest example of a new Russian strategic nuclear system reflecting a policy decision was the introduction and extensive deployment of the single-RV (reentry vehicle) SS-25 and SS-27 ICBM missiles in both silo and mobile basing. The introduction was tied to general agreement between the United States and the Soviet Union to move toward systems that were "stabilizing" in the formal sense of first-strike stability—and were paired with explicit commitments to draw down silo-based systems (particularly the SS-18 missile and the United States MX missile) that heavily used multiple independently targetable reentry vehicles (MIRVs).

With the U.S. withdrawal from the ABM Treaty, Russia abandoned START II and declared that it would retain its MIRVed systems. In addition, in subsequent statements on the future of its missile forces, authorities have made particularly strong statements on their intent to remove the single-RV Topol from the inventory on expiration of its relatively short service life in favor of both older and newer MIRVed systems. The SS-25 missiles will continue to be dismantled as their service lives expire.[53] Deployments of mobile SS-27M missiles were to end in late 2009. But in early 2010, an announcement was made that two more regiments of single warhead SS-27s would be deployed in 2010 (one silo-based in Tatishchevo and one mobile in Teykovo).[54]

The follow-on to these systems began deployments after START I formally expired in December 2009. As of July 2010, one division of RS-24 missiles had been deployed.[55] The RS-24 is fundamentally a MIRVed SS-27M system, with the exact number of warheads unclear (most likely three or four).[56] In addition, as noted, older systems will also be kept around. Official statements in 2009 indicate that Russia will continue dismantlement of SS-18 MUTTH missiles, SS-19 missiles, and SS-25 missiles as the service lives of these systems expire. However, while officials have been explicit about plans to dismantle SS-25s and SS-18 MUTTHs, they have spoken less about the SS-19s.[57] It is therefore possible that some SS-19 missiles might also be retained

---

[53] "Novosti v Rosii," *Vozdushno-Kosmicheskaia Oborona*, No. 3, 2009b, pp. 26–31.

[54] "Novosti v Rosii," 2009b; "RVSN Perevooruzhaiutsia," *Nezavisimoe Voennoe Obozrenie*, June 16, 2009a; *Voenno-Promyshlenyi Kur'er*, "RVSN Segodnia i Zavtra," April 22, 2009; Paul Podvig, "Rocket Forces Tell About Plans for 2009," Russian Strategic Nuclear Forces website (russianforces.org), April 10, 2009b; Paul Podvig, "Second Topol-M Regiment in Teykovo," Russian Strategic Nuclear Forces website (russianforces.org), March 1, 2010a.

[55] "Perviy Division Raket RS-24 Zastupil na Boevoe Dezhurstvo v RF," *RIA Novosti*, July 19, 2010. See also Paul Podvig, "Le RS-24 Est Arrivé," Russian Strategic Nuclear Forces website (russianforces.org), July 19, 2010b.

[56] "Novosti v Rosii" 2009b; *Nezavisimoe Voennoe Obozrenie*, "RVSN Perevooruzhaiutsia," June 16, 2009; "RVSN Segodnia i Zavtra," *Voenno-Promyshlenyi Kur'er*, April 22, 2009; and Paul Podvig, "Rocket Forces Tell About Plans for 2009," Russian Strategic Nuclear Forces website (russianforces.org), April 10, 2009.

[57] "Novosti v Rosii," 2009b.

until 2020, although their service lives are unlikely to support their continuing in service much after that. Moreover, the SS-18 M2s have undergone service life extension to last up to another decade.[58] Officials have even spoken of developing a follow-on to this missile and maintaining a contingent of SS-18s at current numbers (there are now about 40 SS-18 M2s deployed). The SS-18 was designed and built by the Yuzhnoye design bureau in Ukraine, and it is difficult to imagine a follow-on being developed by Russian indigenous firms only. However, Russia does retain agreements with the Ukrainian government and Yuzhnoye that, officials argue, will support the maintenance of existing systems and the development of a follow-on.[59]

Specifically, this suggests that Russian force structure planning for the SRF is based at least in part on a view of stability, as defined by a Russian capacity to defeat U.S. missile defense in a second strike following a U.S. "bolt-from-the-blue" attack. That is, Russia defines stability based on what its weapons can do in a second strike without strategic warning, in an ungenerated posture. While the United States has felt that survivability was best guaranteed by naval systems, Russian planners have tended to put their faith in road-mobile missiles.[60] Military officials make clear that a primary element of deterrent capacity is the ability to overcome missile defenses, an ability that they generally claim Soviet forces currently have and must retain.[61] Discussions of retaining the SS-18 weapon longer than previously planned, and even developing a follow-on for it, as well as the justification for the

---

[58] "Novosti v Rosii," *Vozdushno-Kosmicheskaia Oborona*, No. 1, 2009a, pp. 26–31.

[59] "Novosti v Rosii," 2009a, 2009b; Andrei Fedorov, "Novoe Prishestvie 'Satany,'" *Lenta.ru*, June 12, 2009; "Zavodskii Brak Sorval Zapusk 'Bulavi,'" *KM-Novosti,* June 3, 2009; and "RVSN Perevooruzhaiutsia," 2009.

[60] Rogov et al. (2010) make this point. See also Korotchenko, 2010. Contrary to this prevailing Russian conventional wisdom, Sirotinin (2010) suggests that air- and sea-based systems are more survivable.

[61] See discussion in Oliker et al., 2009. See also Aleksandr Pinchuk, "Obshchestvennyi Sovet—Na Baze RVSN," *Krasnaia Zvezda*, No. 105, June 17, 2009, p. 4.

RS-24 and the Bulava naval missile, similarly focus on these systems' capacity to defeat missile defense.[62]

Strategic Aviation

It is more difficult to assess Russia's plans for its bombers, which seem primarily focused on maintaining the nuclear capability. Most existing Tu-95s are 17 to 24 years old, and many should go out of service by 2015. Russia's Kh-55SM cruise missiles are also aging, and while a new missile has long been in development, it has yet to be deployed. On the other hand, the aircraft have low flying hours and could conceivably be retained for up to 40 years. Fundamentally, Russia will have to decide, in part in the context of treaty negotiations, just how many of these aircraft to retain.[63]

Russia has been putting its Tu-160 bombers (some of which are 24 years old, but one of which was produced only last year) through a modernization that will, among other things, enable these aircraft to be armed with conventional weapons and extend their service life. Russia has spoken of increasing its Tu-160 force by one or two planes per year, getting to 30 by 2030. However, the record of past production is that aircraft have been slow to build and deploy. The newest Tu-160 bomber, which joined the force in 2008, was the first one produced since 2004. Two more Tu-160s were promised by the end of 2009 but have yet to join the force. This demonstrated performance raises questions as to whether any increases will be possible.[64] Entirely new models are even farther off. In 2009, the Defence Ministry contracted

---

[62] "Zavodskii Brak Sorval Zapusk 'Bulavi,'" 2009; Fedorov, 2009. It is worth noting that while the RS-24 appears to be a successful program, the Bulava is experiencing significant setbacks in testing.

[63] Paul Podvig, "Tu-95 MS Go Through Modernization," Russian Strategic Nuclear Forces, www.russianforces.org, July 5, 2008b; Paul Podvig, "Strategic Aviation," Russian Strategic Nuclear Forces website (russianforces.org), April 3, 2009a.

[64] Podvig, 2008b; Paul Podvig, "Russia Added New Tu-160 to Its Bomber Force," Russian Strategic Nuclear Forces website (russianforces.org), April 28, 2008c; Viktor Baranets, "Pochemu Rossiiskoi Armii Ne Khvataet Novogo Oruzhiia?" *Komsomol'skaia Pravda*, June 18, 2009; "Dal'niaia Aviatsiia Zamenit Tu-160 i Tu-22M3 Novym Bombardirovshchikom," *Lenta.ru*, December 12, 2009.

with Tupolev to develop a new bomber, one based on the Tu-160 but utilizing stealth technology. The deployment of the new aircraft is not expected until 2025–2030.[65]

Strategic Nuclear Naval Deployments

Meanwhile, naval nuclear planning and weapon development have faced a number of setbacks. The long-in-development Borei submarine and its Bulava missile, based on the SRF's SS-27M, have been heralded as the basis of Russia's future submarine force. The Delta III submarines are going out of service. Of Russia's three remaining Typhoons, one has been converted to a test platform for the Bulava, and the other two have long been awaiting their fate. In 2009, officials announced that the Typhoons will be retained, but in a conventional role. The Delta IV submarines, now being overhauled and refitted for the Sineva missile (five of the six submarines have completed this process), are in fine shape but are scheduled to be retired by 2017, to be superseded and replaced by the Borei.[66]

The first Borei submarine took over a decade to build—first laid down in 1996, it only went to sea in 2009. The submarine seems to be doing well in its sea trials so far,[67] but the long construction period speaks to the difficulties Russia's navy continues to experience, even with funding up sharply in recent years.[68] (Deputy Prime Minister Sergei Ivanov said recently that the navy receives 40 percent of the defense budget, with the bulk of that going to the strategic subma-

---

[65] "Dal'niaia Aviatsiia Zamenit Tu-160 i Tu-22M3 Novym Bombardirovshchikom," 2009. See also Paul Podvig, "Stealth Plans," Russian Strategic Nuclear Forces website (russian-forces.org), December 22, 2009c.

[66] "Only 8 Russian Strategic Submarines Are Combat-Ready—Analyst," *Johnson's Russia List*, No. 101, June 1, 2009, citing *RIA Novosti*; "Ispytaniia 'Bulavy' Prodolzhatsia" *Voenno-Promyshlennyi Kur'er*, No. 28, July 22, 2009. p. 1.

[67] Viktor Miasnikov, "Ispytaniia 'Bulavy': Opiat' Samolikvidatziia," *Nezavisimaia Gazeta*, July 17, 2009.

[68] Baranets, 2009; and Aleksandr Khramchikhin, "VMF RF Na Zarubezhnikh Korabliakh," *Nezavisimoe Voennoe Obozrenie*, July 3, 2009b.

rine program.[69]) Russian shipbuilding has been a substantial problem and subject of much criticism. That said, the Borei was also delayed when its originally planned missile system, the BARK, was canceled and replaced by the Bulava. The second Borei submarine, laid down in 2004 and promised for 2009, has yet to be completed as of September 2010.[70] It remains to be seen whether the third, laid down in 2006, will meet its production schedule and be complete by 2011. A fourth submarine was to be laid down by the end of 2009, but this was postponed to 2010.[71]

Russian officials, who once spoke of deploying the Boreis in the double digits, first reduced stated plans to eight submarines.[72] In 2009, Deputy Prime Minister Ivanov said that as many would be built as financing allowed, a somewhat ominous statement.[73] At the same time, however, officials have spoken of serial production of the submarine and the Bulava missile.

The Bulava missile has had even worse problems than the submarine. Of 12 tests to date, only one has been deemed fully successful, and seven, including one on September 12, 2009, were clear failures.[74] An October 7 test launch from the submarine *Dmitry Donskoy* to Kamchatka was reported as a success; subsequent planned tests have been delayed. Officials continued to speak of the missile's deployment with the new submarine for tests by the end of 2009, but this did not happen, and there has been much speculation that the missile is

---

[69] "L'vinaia Dolia Biudzheta MO Idet VMF, v Ocnovnom IAdernym Silam—Ivanov," *RIA Novosti*, June 3, 2009.

[70] "Vazhnyi Etap 'Aleksandra Nevskogo,'" *Korabel*, June 16, 2009.

[71] "Zakladka Chetvertoi APL 'Borei' Perenositsia na Pervii Kvartal 2010 Goda," *RIA Novosti*, December 15, 2009.

[72] Iurii Barsukov, "Minoborony Poluchilo Novuiu Tekhniku," *Infox.ru Novie Novosti*, June 17, 2009.

[73] "Chislo Submarin Tipa 'Iurii Dolgorukii' Budet Zaviset' ot Finansirovaniia," *Lenta.ru*, June 3, 2009.

[74] Miasnikov, 2009; "Ispytaniia 'Bulavy' Vozobnoviatsia do Kontsa Mesiatsa," *RIA Novosti,* September 8, 2010.

a failure.[75] On July 22, 2009, the director and general designer of the Bulava's design bureau resigned.[76]

While some have speculated that, in the event of the Bulava's failure, the Borei could be retrofitted for the Sineva missile, officials have said this would be too costly and time-consuming a project. Others have speculated that the Typhoons, which can carry either missile, will be brought back to a nuclear role.[77] Government and industry officials and many specialists, however, insist that there is simply no alternative to the Bulava.[78]

The other issue Russia's submarine force presents is that of patrols and operations. Submarines are only survivable if they are on patrol. Russia's naval operations have deteriorated no less than its shipbuilding. While Russian submarine patrols have increased somewhat recently, it is sobering to note that this increase has meant a total of ten patrols in 2008, especially given that Russian strategic fleet submarines, even when they do go out to sea, generally stay near port.[79] Unless Russia is able to increase its submarine operating tempo and construction, the utility of its submarine force as a useful deterrent will be compromised, regardless of its size and structure. This, of course, aligns with a Russian view of stability as relying on the second-strike capability of its land-based nuclear forces.

---

[75] "Ispytaniia 'Bulavy' Prodolzhatsia" *Voenno-Promyshlennyi Kur'er*, No. 28, July 22, 2009, p. 1.

[76] "Konstruktor 'Bulavi' Podal v Otstavku Iz-Za Neudachnogo Puska Rakety," July 22, 2009.

[77] "Nachal'nik Genshtaba VS RF Nikolai Makarov: 'Bulava' Dolzhna Poletet," *Nauka I Tekhnologii Rossii—STRF.ru*, June 16, 2009; "Zavodskii Brak Sorval Zapusk 'Bulavi,'" 2009; Yuri Zaitsev, "Bulava-M: Still Far from Flying," *RIA Novosti*, September 8, 2005; "Golovami Otvetiat," *Vzgliad*, April 10, 2009.

[78] See the discussion with Yurii Solomonov in Korotchenko, 2010.

[79] Paul Podvig, "Ten Missile Submarine Patrols in 2008," Russian Strategic Nuclear Forces website (russianforces.org), February 17, 2008a.

Russia's Future Force Structure and the New START Agreement

The new START agreement signed by Presidents Medvedev and Obama in April 2010 limits each country's strategic nuclear forces to 1,550 warheads and 800 launchers (deployed or undeployed, with a limit of 700 on deployed launchers). The launcher limit counts each individual ICBM, SLBM, and heavy bomber as one launcher. The warhead limit counts individually RVs on deployed ICBMs and SLBMs and counts each deployed heavy bomber as holding a single warhead, regardless of how many bombs or cruise missiles it might actually carry. The treaty imposes no limits on how each side comprises its force, and the treaty limits are to be reached (that is, reduced in size) by seven years after the treaty's entry into force.[80]

If Russia simply eliminates the forces it is currently planning to eliminate, it will easily be in compliance with the treaty. However, because it is planning to deploy new forces as it draws down old ones, it will have to calculate how the numbers add up to ensure compliance by the treaty deadline. Specifically, Russia must decide whether its force structure plans will assume success, failure, or partial success of the Borei/Bulava program. If it plans on large numbers of Borei submarines equipped with Bulava missiles, these will quickly eat up its warhead, although not its launcher, numbers: Eight Borei submarines can carry up to 1,280 warheads, if the missiles are armed with ten warheads apiece (current plans indicate six warheads apiece, for a total of 768 warheads). If it assumes a smaller number of Boreis, or no Boreis, then a portion of the warhead numbers that could otherwise be allocated to submarines can go to the strategic rocket forces. For example, if the Borei fails, one option is to keep the Delta IV submarines in service longer. If that happens, and the Typhoons are not brought back, Russia's SLBM force will consist of six Delta IV submarines carrying a total of 384 warheads.

---

[80] Dmitry Medvedev and Barack Obama, "Treaty Between the United States of America and the Russian Federation on Measures for the Further Reduction and Limitation of Strategic Offensive Arms," signed April 8, 2010. Bomber counting rules have always required this sort of counting rule with demonstrations of loadings. This new rule favors retention of bombers within the strategic force.

While there are any number of ways to recalculate force numbers, particularly given options for the numbers of warheads on missiles, new START limitations, the challenges that Russia's naval systems face, and the Russian tendency to believe that mobile rocket forces provide greater stability, it seems probable that Russia will seek to approach treaty limits in the future by building more MIRVed ICBMs, particularly the road-mobile RS-24 system. Only if the submarine programs become more successful are the Russians likely to lower the RV count on some missiles. While strategic rocket force deployments have lagged plans, they have not done so by as much as naval forces. This indicates a strong likelihood that Russia's strategic triad will be lopsided in favor of the rocket force component. As noted above, many Russian analysts see this as the more stable posture. However, also as noted, some disagree, and U.S. decisionmakers and analysts will have to consider how stable they consider the combination of Russia's evolving posture with U.S. strategic force development plans. It is also worth noting that, with its emphasis on MIRVed systems, Russia will likely have significantly fewer launchers than the United States, even if approximate parity in warhead numbers is achieved.

Early Warning[81]

Any calculation of strategic stability should not limit itself to just strategic forces structure. As the Russian analyses discussed previously indicate, early warning is an important component of the strategic stability equation. As those articles hint, Russia's early warning system is not in the best of shape. As of the time of this writing, its space component is down to two operational HEO satellites. These satellites are limited in their capacity to detect launches from anywhere other than U.S. territory (including from sea), and they do not have coverage of U.S. territory for more than half of each day. Previously, the HEO constellation

---

[81]   This section draws heavily on Paul Podvig, ed., *Russian Strategic Nuclear Forces*, Cambridge, Mass.: MIT Press, 2004; and Paul Podvig, "Early Warning," Russian Strategic Nuclear Forces website (russianforces.org), September 2, 2010c. The latter piece provides substantial additional information regarding the system. The "Early Warning" section of Podvig (2004) shows coverage diagrams for the highly elliptical orbit (HEO) satellites and gives a history of the development of both the HEO and geosynchronous satellites.

has included as many as nine satellites to ensure reliability and constant coverage of the U.S. land-based missile fields. In the past, the warning system also included geosynchronous satellites that also covered the U.S. Minuteman fields. There are no geosynchronous satellites now in place to observe the Minuteman fields. There are no satellites of any sort configured to detect U.S. SLBM launches from either the Atlantic or the Pacific SSBN patrol areas. A new satellite system is planned but has not yet been fully tested.

Russia also has nine early warning radar stations. These radars can detect incoming ICBM and SLBM RVs but provide much less warning time than launch-detection satellites. Many of these systems are old (built before the 1980s), and although each system has at least one operational radar, two radars (one in Russia and one in Kazakhstan but used by Russia) are not operational. Some new radars have been brought into service to replace those located in former Soviet republics. A radar of the Moscow missile defense system also supports early warning. That system, which came into service in 1995, includes the radar, a command center, and short-range (but no long-range) interceptors. The early warning radar network is also used for space surveillance of objects on low earth orbits. The space surveillance system also includes X-band space surveillance radars (one system, with another planned). Optical observations are used to monitor high-altitude orbit objects.

Until new satellite systems are brought into service that not only cover the U.S. Minuteman fields but also can detect launches of the now hard-target-capable Trident missiles, Russia does not have more than a few minutes of tactical warning from the remaining elements of the early warning system. Repopulating an expanded satellite network would be the first step toward supporting launch under attack as a credible threat.

Other Nuclear Systems

The Intermediate-Range Nuclear Force (INF) Treaty removed entire classes of existing nuclear and conventional weapons from both the Soviet and the U.S. forces (and, by a unilateral action, from the West German forces as well). The removal was accompanied by an intrusive inspection and verification regime to assure both sides that weapons had been removed from the forces and physically destroyed. The treaty further banned the development or deployment of any new weapons of the prohibited types (ballistic missiles and ground-launched cruise missiles with ranges between 500 and 5,500 kilometers). The treaty does not constrain air-launched weapons.

A variety of Russian commentators and occasional military figures have pronounced a need for Russia to withdraw from the INF Treaty and introduce a new class of SS-20-like systems. The SS-20 had a 5,500-kilometer range with three large-yield weapons that had been capable of ranging the whole of the Western TVD (*teatr voennykh deistvii*, or theater of military action or operations). Despite the calls for renunciation of the treaty, the Russian government has not denounced the treaty and there are no indications of development of SS-20-class systems.

Some of the key nuclear systems related to mounting a theater nuclear threat in Europe are controlled not by formal treaties but by "politically binding" statements that were adopted with START to resolve outstanding controversies. The first of these resolved whether the Tu-22M (NATO Backfire) bomber should be counted as a strategic system. The United States accepted that the bomber would not be counted as strategic; the Soviets declared limits on the numbers of aircraft that would be acquired and agreed that they would not equip the aircraft for aerial refueling. The second declaration resolved the question of long-range sea-launched cruise missiles (SLCMs) in a way that was quite different from the highly intrusive inspections agreed for land-based missiles. Long-range SLCMs were defined as missiles of range greater than 600 kilometers. Both sides declared they would deploy no more than 880 such systems and that there would be an annual confidential data exchange detailing the classes of ships that carried such weapons. With these declarations, no inspections of deployed systems were required as part of the overall verification package.[82]

The new military geography of Europe as the Soviet, now Russian, forces have moved back from the old intra-German border to the boundary of Russia itself means that many of the nuclear weapons that remain in tactical inventories simply do not have the range to cover key NATO facilities still located in the old NATO bastions. Tactical weapons can cover targets in the new NATO members, but the principal bases that would support American aircraft waging "contactless war" are well out of range of the less-than-500-kilometer tactical missiles. Figure 3.1 shows the missile range lines from the old East-West Cold War boundary; Figure 3.2 shows the missile range lines from the Russian border; and Figure 3.3 shows the missile range lines from the isolated Russian Kaliningrad enclave that is the home port of the Russian Baltic Fleet.

Leadership Views on Nuclear Force Developments and Posture

While Russian leaders are clear in their statements about the importance of nuclear forces, the actual fortunes of the nuclear program have been variable. Today, Russian officials have made numerous commitments to continued spending on the SRF and naval nuclear forces. The SRF have consistently run at about 6 percent of the defense order.[83] The defense order (procurement) varies from year to year, but runs at about 500 billion rubles annually, depending on what other security forces are included in it. Thus, the SRF are allocated about 30 billion rubles per year. But budgets do not always translate into effective systems.

In recent years, even with substantial resources allocated to the ICBM force, Russia has not built more than ten missiles per year. It is not entirely clear, therefore, whether it will be able to meet its new production and deployment schedule demanding the construction of both

---

[82] U.S. Congress, 102nd Cong., 1st Session, "Message from the President of the U.S. Transmitting the START Treaty, Signed at Moscow on July 31, 1991, Including the Treaty Text, Annexes on Agreed Statements and Definitions, Protocols on Conversion or Elimination, Inspections, Notifications, Throw-weight, Telemetry, JCIC, and the MOU," U.S. Senate Treaty Doc. 102-20, November 25, 1991.

[83] "RVSN Perevooruzhaiutsia," 2009a.

Figure 3.1
Cold War Military Alliances: Ranges of Missiles Deployed in East Germany,
Czechoslovakia, and Hungary

■ Founding members of NATO 1949
▨ Entry: Greece and Turkey 1952, West Germany 1955, Spain 1982
■ Founding members of the Warsaw Pact 1955
▨ Entry: East Germany 1956
▨▨ Withdrawal: Albania 1968

RAND *MG1075-3.1*

Figure 3.2
Ranges of Missiles from Russian Border Following Dissolution of the Warsaw Pact

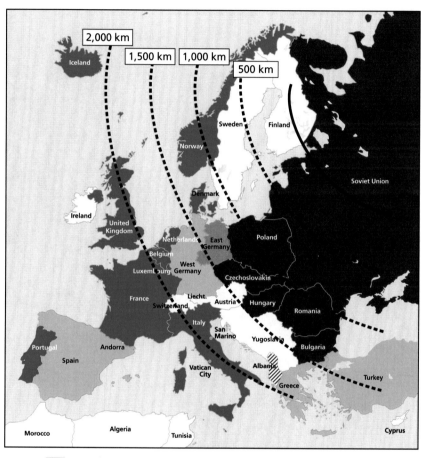

Founding members of NATO 1949
Entry: Greece and Turkey 1952, West Germany 1955, Spain 1982
Founding members of the Warsaw Pact 1955
Entry: East Germany 1956
Withdrawal: Albania 1968

Figure 3.3
Ranges of Missiles Deployed from Kaliningrad Following Dissolution of the Warsaw Pact

Founding members of NATO 1949
Entry: Greece and Turkey 1952, West Germany 1955, Spain 1982
Founding members of the Warsaw Pact 1955
Entry: East Germany 1956
Withdrawal: Albania 1968

RS-24s and (possibly) SS-18 follow-ons. The construction of different missiles at different facilities may help, but, in a weak economy, it is not certain that Russia will be able to maintain substantial funding to the nuclear forces. Recent Russian funding priorities for its security forces are focused on creating capable conventional forces for internal, local, and regional conflict. Combined with an expensive and increasingly unpopular military reform program, it is not clear that the nuclear forces will get the resources they seek.

One critical factor for the future of Russia's nuclear arsenal is how it is seen by the security leadership. For this, lessons lie in the past, which presents a personalized version of policy identified in the rise and fall of individuals known to personify particular approaches or policy positions. This has been especially true in the rise and fall of personalities associated with the strategic nuclear forces. Under Boris Yeltsin, the nuclear forces, as represented by the SRF, reached their peak influence with the appointment of General Igor Sergeev, then commander of the SRF as an independent service, to be Minister of Defence in 1997. Sergeev emphasized the role and modernization of the strategic nuclear forces. He combined the SRF with the Space Forces and sought to unify the SRF, the nuclear missile submarines, and the long-range bombers into a single service—the Strategic Deterrent Force. His investment decisions favored the nuclear forces to the detriment of the conventional forces (naval, ground, and air). Throughout much of his tenure, Sergeev was in public disputes with his Chief of the General Staff, General of the Army Anatoly Kvashnin, the general who earlier in his career had commanded the disastrous December 1994 first foray into Grozny in the First Chechen War and was committed to rebuilding the conventional forces.

Sergeev's ascendancy was brief. By 2001—with Yeltsin's departure and Putin's arrival into the presidency, the experience of the Second Chechen War building on the first, and NATO's intervention in Kosovo—the brief ascent of the nuclear forces was over. Sergeev was dismissed as Minister of Defence. The new Minister of Defence, Sergei Ivanov, a protégé of Vladimir Putin with origins in the Federal Security Service, also had public disputes with Kvashnin, who was sacked along with others after an embarrassing terrorist incursion into Ingushetia.

Key organizational changes followed these departures. Many of these changes simply reversed the changes introduced by Minister of Defence Sergeev. The intended unification to create the Strategic Deterrent Force disappeared. The union of the SRF and the Space Forces was dissolved. The SRF themselves were demoted from a separate service to a separate branch subordinate to the General Staff.

With the promotion of Sergei Ivanov from the Defence Ministry to Deputy Prime Minister in 2007, the personalities associated with defense now include a Minister of Defence with a wholly civilian background, Anatoly Serdyukov, and military officials from traditional backgrounds. A little over a year after Serdyukov took on his new job, Chief of the General Staff Yuri Baluevsky resigned. Baluevsky had served in that position since 2004 and had seen the role of the General Staff as having a substantial analytical component. He had made comments during his tenure indicating deep ambivalence about relations with NATO, raising the possibility of military action in the case of Georgian or Ukrainian NATO membership and emphasizing the possibility of a preemptive Russian nuclear strike (in the event of a threat to the sovereignty and territorial integrity of Russia and its allies, a formulation perfectly in line with Russia's doctrine of the time and since).[84] Baluevsky was replaced by General Nikolai Makarov, who already held, and remained in, the post of First Deputy Minister of Defence. Makarov is a ground-force officer who began his military career in the Group of Soviet Forces in Germany and progressed through the traditional schools, staff positions, and military district command, apparently without acquiring combat experience along the way. His last assignment before becoming the Chief of the General Staff was as Chief of Armament and (as noted) Deputy Minister of Defence within the Ministry of Defence. Makarov's deputy, Colonel General Alexander Kolmakov, is a veteran of the Airborne Forces who emerged from the Ryazan Airborne Academy to early service with the

---

[84] Stephen J. Blank, *The NATO-Russia Partnership: A Marriage of Convenience or a Troubled Relationship?* Carlisle, Pa.: Strategic Studies Institute, 2006; "Russian Chief of Staff Warns Against NATO Expansion," *Georgian Daily*, April 11, 2008; Associated Press, "Russia Says Could Use Nuclear Weapons," January 20, 2008.

Soviet contingent in Afghanistan. This service is tersely described in his posted official biography as "Alexander Kolmakov took part in combat operations with Soviet Forces Afghanistan." Kolmakov progressed through command positions within the airborne forces and military districts. His last position before becoming First Deputy was as Commander of the Airborne Forces.[85]

Together, the Makarov and Kolmakov team exemplifies the complementary skills necessary to plan and organize the ground forces both as a staff enterprise and as an ongoing training and manning effort. Neither of these key men has had any noted association with the strategic nuclear forces during their careers.

In this context, the statements by Security Council Secretary Patrushev (to whom Baluevsky is now a deputy) prior to the publication of the new doctrine are particularly interesting. Was there a debate among the senior leadership regarding possible roles of nuclear weapons that the new doctrine forced to a conclusion? If so, the apparent victory of a more limited role for the weapons, as described in the published doctrine, may indicate a substantial step away from previous thinking.

Major Exercises and Scenarios

In the immediate post-Soviet era, Russia's ability to carry out large military exercises was limited by the need to reorganize forces to match them to the new environment, and by the demands of the war in Chechnya. Nevertheless, there have been large exercises that give insight into the contemporary thinking of the Russian political-military elites. Over the past few years, with the easing of Russia's financial situation, more resources have been devoted to large exercises. This section looks at exercises focused on Europe and Russia's associated signaling to the

---

[85] This section is based solely on the official biographies offered on the Russian Ministry of Defence website (Russian Ministry of Defence, website, no date-a).

United States and NATO, as well as one recent Asia-focused exercise of particular interest.[86]

In 1999, Zapad-99, a major exercise using *Zapad* (West)—the traditional Soviet name of the exercise against NATO—involved forces of the Leningrad and Moscow military districts, the Kalingrad rayon, the Baltic fleet, and the 37th Air Army (formerly Long Range Aviation) together with the military of Belarus. While the exercise took place shortly after the NATO operations in Kosovo, Zapad-99 had been scheduled and announced long before the Kosovo operations. The exercise highlighted the vulnerability of the Kaliningrad enclave (the base of the Russian Baltic fleet), geographically isolated from the rest of Russia and strategic deployment requirements. A key characteristic of the postulated adversary was an ability to conduct mass air attacks with precision weapons. During the exercise itself, Russian spokesmen denied that nuclear weapon release was simulated in the exercise. After the exercise, Defence Minister Sergeev stated that the exercise involved the use of nuclear weapons when conventional weapons failed. Subsequent reports described the exercise as including cruise missile strikes from Blackjack aircraft against targets in theater and the United States.[87]

In January and February 2004, Russia conducted an exercise titled Security-2004 (defined as "command and staff training" rather than a "maneuver" exercise) that was described by contemporary Russian sources as the largest exercise in 20 years. The exercise received

---

[86] In the post-Soviet era, Russia has carried out other exercises with other purposes than influencing the United States or NATO. The series of Russian-Chinese exercises Peace Mission-2005, -2007, and -2009 were joint operations under the aegis of the Shanghai Cooperation Organization that worked out some of the interoperability problems of different languages and systems while simultaneously giving the Russians a chance to demonstrate the latest high-technology systems in pursuit of export contracts. The exercises are conducted jointly by Russian and Chinese forces with observer participation by the other members of the Shanghai Cooperation Organization. Caucasus-2008 was a more ominous exercise with a scenario that featured rapid force deployments to rescue Russian peacekeepers in peripheral deployments. Part threat to the Georgians and part actual rehearsal for the Russian forces, Russian forces moved directly into the Georgian operation as the exercise concluded.

[87] Zapad-99 is described at length in Jacob W. Kipp and Nikolai Sokov, "Chronology of Significant Military Maneuvers," Nuclear Threat Initiative, August 2004.

little notice in the West. This was assisted by Russian discretion in limiting the size and geography of the exercise to avoid triggering Treaty on Conventional Armed Forces in Europe obligations for notifications and observers. The exercise introduced several new features that were not present in the 1999 exercise. A scenario based on "terrorist attack" from the east, south, west, and northwest led eventually to moving ground forces across military district boundaries east of the Urals and reinforcement of the Leningrad military district from the Moscow military district operating along the axis of the Cold War Northwest TVD. The Russian Navy attempted and failed to launch SS-N-23s from a *Delta IV* class submarine, apparently with then-President Putin one of the spectators. Along with multiple flights of Blackjack and Bear bombers launching cruise missiles, the stars of the exercise included the large cruiser *Peter the Great* launching missiles against incoming cruise missile targets, the launch of two ICBMs (Topol and SS-19) by the SRF, and a satellite launch by the Space Forces. The Topol launch from Plesetsk to the Kamchatka Range was supposedly the first to demonstrate a new RV capable of high speed and maneuver to avoid ballistic missile defense interceptors. Despite claims that the exercise was aimed at "terrorists" and not oriented against the United States, a press conference with Deputy Chief of the General Staff Colonel General Baluevsky did evoke the admission that "one does not fight Bin Laden with strategic missiles."[88]

The Stability-2008 exercise running from September 22 to October 21, 2008, was conducted with great fanfare and positive effort to convey the scope of the project shortly after the Georgian conflict concluded. The exercise was described as a strategic exercise within which other levels of exercise were carried out. As the exercise began, an early press release of the Defence Ministry gave an extensive list of the federal executive bodies and military organizations that would be involved:

> The *Stability-2008* strategic command staff exercises involve military command bodies, troops, and military commissariats from the Moscow and Far East military districts, the Baltic, Northern,

---

[88] Sokov, 2004.

and Pacific Fleets, the 11th Air Force and Air Defence Army, the 16th and 37th Air Force Armies, the 32nd Air Defence Corps, the Strategic Missile Troops and the Space Troops, units and organizations of the [Russian Ministry of Defence] logistic forces, operative groups from the federal executive authorities, as well as command bodies and units from the Belarusian Armed Forces.[89]

The Black Sea Fleet and the Caucasus Military District were noticeably absent from the list of participants, having just completed their own live-fire exercise. Units identified in the Stability-2008 exercise included the air component of the Far East MD (11th Air and Air Defense Army), the Tactical Air Army deployed around Moscow (16th Air Army), the Air Defense interceptor aircraft of 32d Air Defense Corps deployed around Moscow, and strategic bombers of the 37th Air Army.[90]

In the exercise scenario, a peripheral conflict gradually escalates with involvement of an outside high-technology adversary. The participation of military commissariats indicates the play of recalling reservists and the evolution toward regional and general war. Despite deployment of forces forward, the situation gradually worsens for the Russian forces and culminates with a variety of strikes, some of them nuclear. Public treatments of the exercises noted sorties from the 37th Air Army, and missile launches by the SRF and ballistic submarines of the Northern Fleet. Bear and Blackjack bombers flew with maximum combat loads and fired the entire load at training ranges, supposedly for the first time since 1984.[91] The Russian Navy redeemed itself after its 2004 failure by launching a Sineva missile from the submarine *Tula* in the Barents Sea to an impact area near the equator in the

---

[89] News Detail, "The Russian Armed Forces Began the Stability-2008 Strategic Command and Staff Exercises," Moscow, September 22, 2008.

[90] The 37th Air Army contains the strategic bombers (Bears and Blackjacks) and also all the Backfire bombers except for a few Russian Naval Aviation aircraft assigned to the Northern and Pacific fleets (the Backfire is sometimes referred to as a Euro-strategic bomber given its range).

[91] Tony Halpin, "Russia to Test Fire Cruise Missiles for First Time Since 1984," *Times Online*, October 6, 2008.

Pacific, a distance of 11,547 kilometers. President Medvedev observed the launch from the Northern Fleet aircraft carrier *Admiral Kuznetsov* with his Defence Minister.

The Stability-2008 exercise marked a high point in openly conducting large exercises with a great deal of publicity and involvement of the political leadership. Exercises in 2009 and 2010, despite being large and sometimes including photo-op involvement of the political leadership, did not offer clear insight into their scenarios or possible nuclear employment. Nor did they enjoy strong affirmation by the political authorities. In the case of the exercises conducted in September 2009, it appears that there was some effort to reduce the visibility of the exercises to foreign audiences and particularly to foreign military observers. In September 2009, a number of purportedly separate exercises were conducted nearly simultaneously and may (or may not) have constituted a single large exercise. By splitting the exercises and keeping the number of troops involved under 13,000 in each of the separate exercises, the Russians have avoided the requirement to invite foreign observers while remaining in formal compliance with their obligations under the agreements of the Organization for Security and Co-operation in Europe (OSCE).[92] Specifically, in 2009, the Ladoga-2009 exercise of the Leningrad Military District was conducted from August 10 to September 28. It overlapped with the joint Belarusian and Russian Zapad-2009 exercise that ran from September 8 to 29. In addition, the SRF conducted an unnamed command-and-staff exercise from September 8 to 11 that involved "operations control in conventional and nuclear warfare" and coincided with the start of the Zapad exercise.[93] The new series of exercises discard the previous Stability label and revive the traditional Zapad (West) label of the Soviet era.

The Zapad-2009 exercise preparations date to early in 2009, when Belarus and Russia announced their agreement on a strategic

---

[92] The relevant obligation for exchange of observers of a military exercise is spelled out in paragraph 47.4 of the Vienna Document (Organization for Security and Co-operation in Europe, *Vienna Document 1999—Of the Negotiations on Confidence- and Security-Building Measures*, November 1999).

[93] "Russia's Strategic Missile Forces to Play War Games on Sept. 8–11," *RIA Novosti*, September 7, 2009.

exercise to be conducted in September 2009. The Zapad-2009 exercise was said to test the interoperability of the Belarusian-Russian regional integrated air defense network agreed between the two countries in February 2009.[94] The exercise scenario also involved movement of Russian ground forces into Belarus. Before the exercise, it was asserted in at least one newspaper that tactical nuclear use would be simulated.[95] Later reports in the same paper asserted no such nuclear scenario, tactical or strategic.[96] However, Tu-160 and Tu-95 strategic bombers took part and overflew the exercise location in Belarus on September 23.[97] Tu-22M3 (Backfire) and Su-24M (Fencer) aircraft also participated in the exercise and conducted live fire with new high-precision systems, presumably conventional, demonstrating rapid retargeting using information from a ground commander.[98] The English-language Russian Ministry of Defence summary at the conclusion of the Zapad exercise refers to the use of "combat and special weaponry," which could arguably be interpreted to indicate the use of nuclear weapons.[99]

The Zapad-2009 scenario, which Russian President Medvedev noted was "purely defensive," simulated a NATO attack on Belarus.[100]

---

[94] "Russia to Conduct Large-Scale War Games in the Fall," *RIA Novosti*, March 10, 2009. The exercise with Belarus will now be conducted every two years.

[95] Iaroslav Viatkin, "Chereda Bol'shikh Uchenii," Argumenty Nedeli, July 10, 2009.

[96] "Chereda Bol'shikh Uchenii," *Argumenty Nedeli*, June 10, 2009.

[97] *Zvezdanews*, "Ucheniia 'Zapad-2009.' Rossiiskie Raketonostzy Pribyli v Belorussiiu," September 23, 2009.

[98] "Russian Bombers Test High-Precision Weaponry During Drills," *RIA Novosti, Baranovochi*, September 27, 2009.

[99] Russian Ministry of Defence, "Press Release of the Incorporated Press Centre of the Operative-and-Strategic Exercise 'Zapad-2009' ('West-2009'), September 30, 2009b. Note that while the English-language version refers to special weaponry, traditionally understood to mean nuclear, the Russian language version refers to "special equipment/technology" (*tekhnika*), which carries no such meaning (Russian Ministry of Defence, "Press-Reliz Ob'edinennogo Press-Tsentra Operativno-Strategicheskogo Ucheniia 'Zapad-2009,'" September 29, 2009a). The release includes a rather extensive list of vehicles and platforms involved in the exercise that legalistically do not exceed the limits given in the Vienna Agreement.

[100] See Roger McDermott, "*Zapad 2009* Rehearses Countering a NATO Attack on Belarus," *Jamestown Foundation Eurasia Daily Monitor*, Vol. 6, No. 179, September 30, 2009.

The exercise details, as revealed in the official news releases, give no insight into whether or how any nuclear weapons were employed in the scenario. Nor do we know what took place in the posssibly associated SRF exercise. Whether through accident or design, the Russian conduct of several exercises with no OSCE observers present had the effect of making the Zapad-2009 exercise much less visible to the United States and the original NATO states than some past exercises. They were, however, quite visible to Poland and the Baltic states by reason of those countries' immediate proximity to the action. It is therefore worth highlighting that Polish accounts of the exercises in the Polish news magazine *Wprost* claimed that the exercise included nuclear strikes and an amphibious assault and attack on a gas pipeline—both presumably in Polish territory. In addition, according to Polish sources, the scenarios supposedly included suppression of an uprising by a national minority in Belarus—a country with a Polish minority that has differences with the regime. A number of Polish members of Parliament felt that Poland was undoubtedly the target of the exercises and were particularly sensitive to the exercise kicking off on the 70th anniversary of the Soviet invasion of Poland in 1939.[101] In much the same way, the Russian-only exercise Ladoga-2009 was seen as taking the borders of Russia with Latvia, Lithuania, and Estonia as a hypothetical front line.[102]

The most recent major exercise at the time of this writing was Vostok-2010, held June 29–July 8 of that year. Although not a Europe-focused exercise, it is included here because it may indeed have had a nuclear component. Ostensibly an exercise developed to test the new organizational structure of the Armed Forces, its scenario involved a fight against illegal armed groups or terrorists. Running counter to the scenario, however, was the size of the Far East effort. The exercise included land, sea, and air components: 20,000 troops, a variety of armored vehicles, artillery, air defense, and other weaponry, 40

---

[101] The *Wprost* story seems to have been picked up in English only in the *Telegraph* (Matthew Day, "Russia 'Simulates' Nuclear Attack on Poland," *Telegraph.co.uk*, November 1, 2009).

[102] Anna Dunin, "Intel Brief: Poland on Edge over Russian Drills," International Relations and Security Network, November 18, 2009.

ships, and 75 aircraft and helicopters (among them Su-24M and Su-24 fighter-bombers). It included response to aerial attack, an amphibious assault force landing, and anti-tank maneuvers. While some speculated that Russian armed forces planners failed to fulfill the Ministry of Defence's directive to focus on small efforts and not simulate major combat, others saw the exercise as a thinly disguised model of a conflict with China.[103] While no strategic nuclear assets were involved, the exercise included what was described in several sources as nuclear weapon use by Russian forces. One formulation referred to a nuclear "fougasse,"[104] another referred to a "low-yield 'nuclear' attack."[105] Note that atomic demolition munitions (which might be one possible explanation/translation) are not generally believed to be in the Russian arsenal.

If the exercise was, indeed, simulating a large-scale attack, particularly one with territorial aspirations, nuclear use (whatever its form) would be in line with the new doctrine. Anything short of that, however, would suggest that the exercise, if it indeed used nuclear weapons, was not aligned with the new doctrine. However, the use of a small-scale nuclear weapon would hardly suggest relying on nuclear use in the face of conventional weakness. Thus, the exercise presents a possible disconnect with both existing doctrine and the direction in which doctrine appeared to be evolving prior to the publication of the new doctrine.

It is also worth noting that the Russian SRF and related components also engage in exercises, such as command-staff exercises and exercises focused on strategic force security.[106] Moreover, defense

---

103 "Serdiukov Ne Velel Ustraivat' Voinu Dvukh Armii," *Nezavisimoe Voennoe Obozrenie*, July 9, 2010; Il'ia Kramnik, "Razmakh Vpechatliaet, A Problemy Trevozhat," *Voenno-Promyshlennyi Kur'er*, July 13, 2010; Oleg Falichev, "'Vostok-2010': Nachalo, Kul'minatsiia, Epilog," *Voenno-Promyshlennyi Kur'er*, July 14, 2010; Khramchikhin, 2010c.

104 Egor Sozaev-Gur'ev Falichev, "Kazaki I Raketchiki Protiv 'Bangrupy,'" *Infox.ru*, July 8, 2010.

105 Valerii Usol'tsev, "Boi Na Sergeevskom Poligone," *Suvorovskii Natisk*, July 17, 2010.

106 "Novosti v Rosii," 2009b; "V Podmoskov'e Proidut Ucheniia Protivodiversionnoi Roty RVSN," *Oruzhie Rosii*, July 14, 2008; "RVSN Provodiat Iadernye Ucheniia," *Golos Rosii*, March 10, 2010.

of nuclear forces has been a component of major exercises, including Vostok-2010.[107] This aligns with Russian concerns expressed in the academic literature that enemies will seek to destroy Russian nuclear capability early in a conflict.

As the discussion above demonstrates, the Cold War era's strong connection between the features of military exercises and those in actual contingency plans can no longer be asserted given the contingent character of the conflict, the relative position of key force elements, and lack of clarity as to whether deployed forces could range desired target sets. Exercises now involve extensive interaction among different levels of command and different military and civilian emergency agencies, and these interactions have resulted in the contingency scenarios developing into nuclear confrontations.

There is also another confounding factor: Exercise designers may be using military exercises to showcase particular service capabilities, in part to influence resource decisions. Indeed, some of the systems identified in the Levshin et al. article as particularly appropriate for use in "de-escalation of military operations" scenarios—such as nuclear SLCMs—have been absent from the public record of the major exercises, while other systems identified as problematic for this mission have gradually become more prominent. The use of both the START-counted strategic bombers (the Tu-95 Bears and Tu-160 Blackjacks) and the "Euro-strategic" Tu-22M Backfire bombers could indicate a possible scenario of mixing in nuclear cruise missiles with others to saturate defenses, thereby masking the nuclear character of an attack until weapon detonation.[108] Alternatively, the involvement of these systems may have had a purely demonstrative purpose.

Table 3.3 shows the systems mentioned in the 1999 Levshin et al. article and those that have been publicly noted in subsequent major exercises. Certainly, part of this difference in weapons employment is

---

[107] "V Ucheniiakh 'Vostok-2010' Primut Uchastie Kosmicheskie Voiska i RVSN," *RIA Novosti*, June 28, 2010.

[108] During the Cold War, the Soviets greatly feared the use of nuclear cruise missiles, particularly in the Western TVD as part of the NATO deployment of Pershing II and GLCM. See Rose E. Gottemoeller, *Land-Attack Cruise Missiles*, London: International Institute for Strategic Studies, 1987.

Table 3.3
Nuclear Platform Appearance in Articles and Exercises

Nuclear Platform	1999 Levshin et al. Article	Zapad-99	Security-2004	Stability-2008	Concurrent Zapad-2009, Ladoga-2009, unnamed SRF	Vostok-2010
Operational-tactical						
Ground force, missile, mine	X					Possible
Frontal and naval aviation	X				Unclear	
Operational-strategic						
SLCM	X					
Strategic bomber	X	X	X	X	Unclear, bombers present	
Strategic						
ICBM			X	X	In concurrent exercise	
SLBM			X	X		

the contrast between the Levshin et al. article's underlying vision and the current Russian understanding of how the conflict would occur. Levshin and his co-authors envisioned a situation much like the old NATO–Warsaw Pact scenario of troops in physical contact, the principal difference from the Cold War era being an expectation of NATO predominance in combat power at the point of contact and movement into and through a Russian defended sector. Over time, it seems that the exercise scenarios have come to place greater emphasis on types of conflict that are closer to "contactless war."

One effect visible in the exercises had been the gradual inclusion of more and more of the strategic forces until the break with the past in Zapad-2009. Even if that exercise, or one of the possibly associated exercises, included a nuclear component, it is clear that those running the exercise and providing official coverage of it do not particularly want to emphasize to either foreign or domestic audiences any nuclear elements of the exercise.

Endorsement by the Political Authorities

Zapad-99 demonstrated the Russian military's recognition that it was outclassed by American and NATO forces and that the Russians might have to use nuclear weapons to ward off conventional defeat. While the demonstration was alarming to Americans who followed the exercise, the political effect of the exercise was undercut by President Yeltsin's post-exercise speech to the participants, in which he thanked them for their efforts but noted in passing that the threat of the exercise was "something for sci-fi books."[109] Clearly, the incident demonstrated a certain lack of harmony between the political and military on what threats Russia faced.

In contrast to Yeltsin's behavior after Zapad-99, President Medvedev treated Stability-2008 and the military commanders who conducted it in a wholly different manner. President Medvedev spoke at the start of the exercise, announcing its start and describing its purpose. He also observed a number of the component exercises, choosing to be photographed in a leather jacket on an aircraft carrier in the Barents Sea while watching an SLBM launch. It is probably not a coincidence that Medvedev was present for the most unambiguously nuclear component of the exercise (just as Putin would have been in the 2004 exercise if the SS-N-23 had successfully launched).[110] Medvedev then journeyed to Kazakhstan for the conclusion of Centre-2008, one of the component exercises of Stability-2008, and the conclusion of the overall exercise. Centre-2008 was a joint exercise with the Kazakh military under the Collective Security Treaty Organization and simulated defense against an incursion into Kazakhstan from the south to a depth of tens of kilometers. In addressing the commanders of the military districts, Medvedev started his speech with an old-style "dear

---

[109] Ilya Bulavinov, *Kommersant-Daily*, July 3, 1999, pp. 1–2, quoted in Kipp, 2001.

[110] While both Medvedev and Putin have been observers of nuclear associated events within the exercises, it does not appear that either has been a participant in the exercises themselves. How current Russian exercises simulate decisionmaking at the civil-military boundary is not described in the public sources. In the 1983 *Able Archer* exercise, one of the most alarming elements from the Soviet perspective was supposedly the recognition that national leaders were involved and exercising nuclear weapon release procedures.

friends" and proceeded to lay out the importance of the Centre-2008 exercise (described as an operational-strategic exercise within the strategic exercise Stability-2008), explaining,

> The name of the exercises speaks for itself and is deeply symbolic today. Stability is precisely what our government is seeking and what we must uphold in a variety of situations, if required by using military force.
>
> Just recently we had to react to the aggression launched by the Georgian regime and, as we have seen, an absolutely real war can erupt suddenly and local simmering conflicts, which are sometimes even called frozen, can turn into a real military fire.[111]

Along with a programmatic list for the development of the armed forces, Medvedev ended his speech by referring to the newly agreed strategic concept, including explicit reference to the 2020 time frame it presents. Medvedev noted that "By 2020 we must guarantee our capacities of nuclear deterrence in various military and political conditions, in various military and political situations, as well as ensure the comprehensive provision of new types of weapons and means of gathering intelligence."[112]

Medvedev also observed both the Zapad-2009 and Vostok-2010 exercises, emphasizing the exercises' defensive nature at the former while leaving it to General Staff Chief Makarov to deliver the same message at the latter. Medvedev made no reported comments regarding either the presence or absence of nuclear escalation in either exercise. Indeed, in the official press coverage of President Medvedev's visit to Belarus at the conclusion of the Zapad-2009 exercise, the military exercise itself was treated as only part of the news. Medvedev's statement that the exercise was of a defensive nature and that the two countries were "not

---

[111] Dmitry Medvedev, "Opening Address at a Meeting with Commanders of Military Districts," September 26, 2008.

[112] Ibid. The expression "frozen conflict" was used for situations such as the placement of peacekeepers in South Ossetia under the Sochi Agreement, in which there was no time set for withdrawal of peacekeepers or termination of the agreement.

threatening anyone" was included in a news release with items such as Russia and Belarus working on a "milk export" dispute.[113]

---

[113] "Russian, Belarusian Leaders to Discuss Trade, Military Ties," *RIA Novosti*, September 29, 2009.

CHAPTER FOUR

An Emerging Russian Deterrent Framework?

Based on the evidence, some inferences can be drawn with respect to the evolving Russian deterrent framework in Europe and elsewhere.

For claimed interests, Russia is using the traditional mechanisms of formal alliances, security treaties, and agreements to joint measures to consolidate its relationship with some of the former member states and portions of the USSR. In addition, the so-called Medvedev Doctrine asserts Russian willingness to protect "privileged interests" and Russian citizens in regions where Russia shares particular historical relations. The doctrine gives fuller expression to behaviors exemplified by the long-standing willingness of the Russians to retain troops in the de facto independent Trans-Dniester that has broken away from the Republic of Moldova, as well as in Abkhazia and South Ossetia. It also implies a willingness to defend its claimed interests with military force. The phrasing may also be intended to ensure that potential military actions to retain and defend privileged interests can be defined as resisting "aggression" and more broadly to retain privileged interests.

We can have much less certainty in inferences about how possible conflicts might develop and how nuclear weapons might figure in their conduct. On the one hand, there is no question that Russian nuclear forces retain a central mission of deterring nuclear (and prospectively conventional) attack by U.S. or other forces. On the other hand, the Russian military is no longer positioned for immediate contact with the main NATO forces. The immediate line of contact with NATO is confined to the Baltic states on Russia's border and the isolated Russian enclave of Kaliningrad. Geography will not permit the immediate contact of large ground forces.

The Russian experience of local wars from Afghanistan to Georgia, and particularly the two Chechen wars, has had a profound effect on its ground forces. Much of the impetus for changing from a conscript force to a professional force has come from the demand for soldiers and, more generally, security forces able to withstand the rigors of such conflicts. This change to a professional force has not, however, thus far included the introduction of new weapon systems for ground forces or configuring the ground forces for large-scale warfare with modern NATO forces.

Looking at Russian exercise scenarios from 1999 to 2008 highlights the quandary of Russian security and conventional forces oriented toward conflict on the country's periphery with opponents such as Georgia or violent extremists. In these exercises, Russia first comes into conflict with such opponents and then, through a chain of unfortunate events, the situation develops into conflict with a larger power (perhaps NATO and/or the United States).[1] The conventional phase of this conflict does not go well and the exercises move toward an apparent Russian first use of nuclear weapons to compensate. This represents a somewhat reluctant use of nuclear weapons at the tail end of an escalation ladder. The Russians are not focused on an opportunity to surprise and defeat but instead seek to ward off defeat by the application of nuclear weapons as a response to, for example, American and NATO conventional precision-strike systems. Which nuclear weapons might be used, how they might be targeted and for what intended effects, and exactly what situations or actions would trigger their employment are contingent on the particulars of the situation. All of this is a marked contrast to the Cold War past, when the leadership believed that in any conflict the movement toward nuclear employment would follow only a few known and recognizable pathways—one of these being the

---

[1]   Or, as in *Vostok-2010*, Russia manages to attain a large-scale conflict with no other countries posited in the scenario at all, although the ostensible bandits possess strikingly state-like capabilities.

"bolt-from-the blue"—that permitted reliance on a relatively few pre-scripted responses to identifiable actions on the part of the adversary.

In Russian thinking, the large intercontinental exchange scenario, similar to those of the past, arises primarily from the prospect of a bolt-from-the-blue attack by the United States. While this continues to remain the focus of much writing, force structure developments and leadership focus do not align with a view of this as a crucial planning factor. The low rate of deployment of ICBMs, the many problems with the submarine program, and, perhaps most importantly, the continuing disrepair of Russia's strategic early warning systems appear to belie the concerns voiced by analysts and some officials. While one might ascribe this to ineptitude, deterioration, and lack of investment in the military-industrial complex, this disconnect remains an anomaly. Large-scale strategic nuclear exchange, moreover, is not the situation that generates the intellectual effort and exercise focus of the conflict-escalation scenarios. These arise from a genuine political crisis and events that are perhaps neither intended nor under the control of either side at the beginning of the conflict. In other words, the defense of privileged interests may include things we might characterize as non-combatant evacuation operations or, certainly from the Russian perspective, defense of citizens of Russian extraction in the near abroad.[2] All of these are problems that might initiate conflict quite different from the Cold War and even the recent post–Cold War. In short: Theater war is undesirable but possible. Some Russian thought has been devoted to the idea that situations can arise in which nuclear weapon use is the unintended end result of a series of actions and decisions taken reluctantly by both sides. More recently, however, this seems to have dropped off, raising the question of whether Russian thinking still posits this to be the case and, if so, under what conditions.

Moreover, despite a political-military situation in Europe that in the past might have invited a revived SS-20-class nuclear missile system as a technological response to the military situation, Russia has

---

[2] An early U.S. Army–sponsored "Army After Next" wargame posited just such a scenario for how U.S. and Russian forces could be brought into conflict in a post–Cold War European context.

not denounced the INF Treaty. The terms of the INF Treaty itself include the actual barring of not just nuclear versions of the system but all ground-based missile weapons of this type, and the terms of the treaty make it fairly easy to assure that neither side has them. This was an arms control milestone. One might think that with the movement from the inter-German border back to the border of Belarus as the defended area, Russian strategic systems (and the nonstrategic nuclear weapons of adequate range, such as Backfires and SLCMs) have to pick up the theater nuclear mission.

The combination of Russia's claimed interests in the states on its periphery and past indications of the possible "thinkability" of theater nuclear war raises the issue of whether, implicitly or explicitly, Russian planning and approaches had been heading in a direction of not only deterring large-scale U.S. attack but also seeking to influence U.S. policy actions in Europe. Such an approach makes sense in many ways. Just as Russia fears that the United States would use a prospective nuclear superiority to influence Russia's policies, Russian nuclear posture and the possibility of nuclear weapon use can be tools to influence U.S. policy, particularly on extending NATO to former Soviet states on Russia's periphery. Russian nuclear forces in this context can be seen as a tool to dissuade further NATO enlargement.

Although this may have been the direction of Russian thinking into 2009, the publication of the new doctrine, coupled with the most recent large-scale exercises, Zapad-2009 and Vostok-2010, suggests that there may have been a change in policy. The possibility that this was the result of extended debate raises the question of whether or not this policy could be reversed yet again—and the answer, as with all policies, is that of course it could. How to interpret possible nuclear use in Vostok-2010, which post-dates the new doctrine, is now more difficult, as the possible nuclear use could be either a vestige of the old doctrine or an application of the new. In the meantime, however, we must consider the meaning of changes to the published doctrine.

A close look at the new doctrine does not show that it is impossible for theater conflict to evolve to nuclear use by Russia. It indicates that the bar may have been raised, but scenarios can still be imagined in which such an evolution takes place. If it is true that Russian planners (like some Russian analysts) see conventional conflict with the United States as impossible because the United States would seek to destroy Russia's nuclear capability, one could argue that the threshold is actually quite low. While this is, in principle, countered by Russian arguments that they would not strike before being attacked, we must wonder what would, and would not, constitute an attack. Moreover, there is no guarantee that any such decisions would be made on the basis of reliable information, given Russian neglect of its early warning and command and control systems.

Also worth considering is the question of Russia's alliance commitments and their implications. For example, some Russian analysts felt that Russian nuclear capability was, at least in part, what prevented U.S. involvement in the August 2008 war between Russia and Georgia.[3] If the new doctrine had been in place then, however, this deterrent would have been far weakened, as the sovereignty and existence of Russia were not at stake. Today, however, with Russia having signed formal alliances with both South Ossetia and Abkhazia, a Georgian (or any other country's) attack on the territory of either or both those regions will without question pose a threat to the existence of a Russian ally or allies. This, of course, would, under the new doctrine (as well as under old doctrines) be an unquestionable justification for the use of nuclear force, if Russia deemed such use to be required.

While this presentation of possible nuclear use is a sobering element, we should remember that Russian authorities in the doctrinal and policy discussions understand the grave risks in consciously precipitating such action and do not seek to have it occur. Nevertheless, the possibility of an unintended conflict rapidly escalating toward an unacceptable outcome must be taken seriously.

---

[3]   Kazennov and Kumachev, 2010.

CHAPTER FIVE

Implications for the United States

In the Cold War era, the most absolute statement of American interests in Europe was the North Atlantic Treaty, particularly Article 5, which states that an armed attack on any of the parties to the treaty in Europe or North America will be considered an attack against them all. NATO created the military-political apparatus to plan and execute any military responses required under the treaty. NATO continues in force and represents the sole existing treaty-level mechanism committing the United States to military responses in Europe. American claims of interests in Europe are most strongly made by the admission of countries to NATO through expansion or American support for admitting particular countries to become future members of NATO. However, actions and statements far short of this are seen in Europe, Russia, and elsewhere as signals of intent to claim interests. In addition, NATO and American willingness to expand military operations to out-of-area commitments expand the possible geographic areas in which NATO and Russia can come into conflict.

Russia's claim of interest in protecting Russian citizens wherever they may be, as well as to countries that have shared historical relations, has implications for U.S. policy. In the absence of formally or informally recognizing these Russian interests, the United States faces the possibility of being drawn into a conflict that, under certain conditions, could escalate to the Russian use of nuclear weapons. Russia itself is rethinking some of its issues and interests in a Eurasian context, rather than a strictly European context, and this creates additional potential disconnects between NATO and Russian situation assessments. Perhaps even more importantly, unless the United States clearly delineates its own goals and commitments on Russia's periphery, the potential for misread signals leading to conflict increases. What this suggests is that the United States should design its own deterrent framework to avoid ambiguous commitments while seeking ways to enhance stability through arms control. The United States should also assess the implications for U.S. military planning and forces, and specifically for the Air Force.

Deterrent Framework

Throughout the Cold War, the fundamental bases of the U.S. deterrent framework with respect to the Soviet Union had two parts: (1) the direct threat of a devastating retaliatory response to a conflict that began with a strategic nuclear attack on the United States and (2) the willingness to extend deterrence to formal allies by the employment of nuclear weapons should other means fail to repel aggression. The second part has been most fully developed in the elaborate mechanisms for nuclear weapon employment developed during the Cold War with the original NATO allies. For much of the Cold War, the expected outcome of nuclear weapon use in-theater was eventual escalation to a general nuclear exchange between the central strategic systems.

So how has the deterrent framework changed? Certainly, the first part of the deterrent framework continues in place: Even as both Russia and the United States profess that war initiating with a central exchange is unlikely and growing more so, one must be concerned about questions of strategic stability as their arsenals evolve, particularly if the two countries' relationship begins to degrade. The second part of the deterrent framework has new complexities. The very success of U.S. and NATO conventional abilities may have changed the circumstances for potential nuclear employment in some cases. It is extremely unlikely, given the current state of forces, that NATO would be compelled to use nuclear weapons because of the failure of its conventional forces to repel aggression. On the other hand, Russia's use of nuclear weapon while losing conventionally or fearing a U.S. attack on its homeland or allies is not addressed fully by existing NATO or American planning or declaratory policy.

To avoid having to decide in the moment how they will respond, the United States and NATO need to plan for the changed military environment and geography in Europe. This raises a broad range of political questions that must be decided by the national leadership of the United States and its NATO allies regarding their commitments and policies in and near Europe and farther into Eurasia as well. With NATO involved in military conflicts in other regions and widespread economic problems, there is no high-level interest in addressing these commitments. In the absence of that high-level policy, lower levels in the hierarchy must plan within the ambiguities of the situation.

Among other things, this means that NATO and the U.S. military and political staffs must maintain an awareness of what sorts of actions and operations raise the risk of a Russian nuclear response or action, and plan their own policies and operations in light of that risk. In some cases, this may mean avoiding certain actions; in others it may require more explicit and direct communication with Russia in planning and preoperational stages than might otherwise be deemed necessary, to prevent misunderstandings and misperceived signals (or actions erroneously viewed as signals) on both sides.

It also means that, absent a commitment to avoid such situations entirely, U.S. and NATO military staffs need a plan for the possible Russian use of nuclear weapons.

In examining the possible role of NATO nuclear weapons in such plans, NATO planners must themselves deal with the changed military geography. Dual-capable aircraft (DCA) are the sole surviving element of in-theater nuclear forces.[1] The nuclear weapons for some NATO aircraft are provided by the United States under bilateral commitments, and the United States retains nuclear weapons for U.S. tactical aircraft. These aircraft would face much longer-range missions in the new geography. Modernizing the aging gravity weapons will

---

[1] This presumes that the United States continues the policy initiated by President George H. W. Bush of keeping Tomahawk land attack missiles—nuclear (TLAM-Ns) off surface ships and submarines.

involve many political and diplomatic sensitivities. As with the Russian employment of its long-range aviation, it may be that if such nuclear missions in the future are necessary, they would best be carried out by strategic platforms.

Enhancing Stability Through Arms Control

Russia's strategic nuclear force developments and U.S. abandonment of the ABM Treaty have undercut the basis for providing strategic stability, as enshrined in START, which called for reducing the heavily MIRVed, highly accurate ICBMs based in silos on both sides.[2] Finding a new basis for stability as nuclear stockpiles are reduced raises new challenges.

The current trend lines of Russian strategic nuclear forces, including an emphasis on MIRVed missiles and a submarine program in trouble, and paired with the limits envisioned in the 2009 Joint Understanding between Presidents Obama and Medvedev, could leave Russia with substantially fewer launchers than the U.S. strategic nuclear force.

Instability arises not simply from force structures, but from perceptions of vulnerabilities and judgments on how a conflict might begin. Thus, if Russia fears *not only* that it is not able to maintain a credible second-strike capability in the face of U.S. missile defenses, but also that an unexpected nuclear attack by the United States is plausible, the incentives for striking first are increased.

The possibility of nuclear employment at the theater level creates a completely different set of stability concerns, suggesting that other

---

2   The large number of weapons available for prompt launch and the ability to target each silo with two or more RVs, with a resulting high probability of destroying a missile with more than two RVs, produces a net advantage for the attacker. A counterforce attack against the opponent's entire ICBM force concentrated in relatively few silos might permit the attacker to greatly reduce the damage that the opponent could inflict in a retaliatory strike, while the attacker retained large numbers of ICBM RVs to threaten utter destruction of the opponent. Both Soviet and U.S. policymakers agreed that this presented an undesirable situation, in which the possible attraction of executing such an attack with the aim of "winning," combined with the possibility of error or inadvertence in adopting a launch on warning posture to negate the effectiveness of such an attack, could actually increase the risk of conflict.

principles may also be in play. Indeed, a theater conflict with possible nuclear use may render the strategic "stability" of some weapon systems suspect as inventory levels are reduced. [3]

In the Cold War, strategic nuclear bombers were viewed as a potential means for signaling escalation as part of intrawar deterrence. In their recent exercises, the Russians have demonstrated employment of strategic bombers for theater nuclear missions as well as the employment of the "Euro-strategic" Backfire bomber. This raises for the United States the question of how to think about its Air Force strategic bombers in such a context, especially in light of their importance to conventional campaigns, the prospective reduction in strategic nuclear weapons, and their potential employment as a platform for nuclear responses to Russian theater nuclear weapon use. For both sides, the generation of the strategic bomber force for the nuclear mission while a conventional conflict is under way might be detectable and yet easily mistaken, since both sides deploy on their bombers cruise missiles that have both nuclear and conventional variants of the same basic airframe. Because of the uncertainty that the other side will get the "message," the utility of the strategic bombers for signaling may be less today than it was in the period when strategic bombers were solely nuclear capable.

The Russians describe their SSBNs as "retaliatory-strike" forces along with the mobile ICBMs—a view expressed as recently as September 5, 2009, by the deputy commander of the SRF.[4] In the context of a conventional conflict with NATO, attrition of Russian submarines, either as a result of intentional strategic antisubmarine warfare or

---

3   The various approaches to "stability" and their explicit and implicit contexts are well described in Charles L. Glaser, "Why Do Strategists Disagree About the Requirements of Strategic Nuclear Deterrence?" in Lynn Eden and Steven E. Miller, eds., *Nuclear Arguments: Understanding the Strategic Nuclear Arms and Arms Control Debates*, Ithaca, N.Y.: Cornell University Press, 1989. The particular conceptions of "stability" important to the START treaty are dealt with in Kerry M. Kartchner, *Negotiating START: The Quest for Stability and the Making of the Strategic Arms Reduction Treaty*, New Brunswick, N.J.: Transaction, 1992.

4   BBC Monitoring, "Russian Strategic Missile Troops General Details Re-Armament, Structure," Ekho Moskvy Radio, September 5, 2009. The interview with Lt Gen Vladimir Gagarin was part of the "Military Council" series that is a joint production with the Russian Defence Ministry's Zvezda TV.

as collateral casualties of war at sea, might by itself add an additional destabilizing element.

How to think about "stability" in the context of a local conflict growing to regional conflict with NATO or U.S. involvement leading to nuclear employment is complicated by the possibility that the bombers and submarines previously thought to be the most stability-inducing elements of the respective strategic triads may no longer function that way (if they ever did in Soviet/Russian thinking). Indeed, the possibility of using a conventional phase to set up the conditions of a strategic exchange or to significantly change the balance of strategic forces figures in some Russian theoretical discussions of the nuclear option in-theater. There is no doubt that, from the very start of the discussion of nonstrategic nuclear weapon use as a counter to conventional weakness, Russian analysts have recognized this as a delicate balance of conscious brinksmanship and have recognized that "controlled, limited nuclear war is not one-sided."[5] Given the current low-alert states of most nuclear weapons, the principal mechanisms of achieving stability in terms of the old criteria of assuring delivery of a retaliatory response would appear to be the generation of the non-alert forces, dispersal of mobile ICBMs on the Russian side, generation and flushing of not-at-sea SSBNs, and the posturing of warning and command and control assets for either assured responses or possible launch under attack.

Given the centrality of Europe to the scenario discussed here, it should not be surprising that the previously negotiated arms control treaties, created expressly to deal with European nuclear issues, are most relevant. The continuance of the INF Treaty—even as Russians claim to be relatively disadvantaged by its continuance—is a positive sign. Whatever transpires, it will be important to negotiate strategic arms control in relation to continued observation of the INF Treaty. Otherwise, from the perspective of usable nuclear weapons and how they are thought of in war, denunciation of the INF Treaty would put more nuclear weapons in situations that the United States is trying to

---

[5]   S. V. Kreydin, quoted in Kipp, 2001. There seems to be an echoing of the original NATO formulation of initial nuclear use threatening progressive loss of control and further escalation.

prevent. There is no advantage, from the American perspective, in reintroducing INF-prohibited systems to Europe.

True long-range air-launched cruise missiles (ALCMs) are already controlled under both START and the Treaty Between the United States of America and the Russian Federation on Strategic Offensive Reductions (SORT, better known as the Moscow Treaty), and their carriers will be controlled under the new START agreement. Existing "politically binding" commitments undertaken with START and understandings on the exchange of information on long-range nuclear SLCMs put some bounds on the possible size and presumable origins of SLCM nuclear attacks. Inclusion of long-range nuclear SLCMs under additional arms control agreements would significantly reduce the size of any potential threat of long-range SLCMs.[6]

Although open to dispute, the present arms control understanding on not counting the Backfire bomber as a strategic system because of its range does set a precedent for performance parameters that might be used for any new Air Force aircraft, such as the "2018 bomber," without triggering claims that the platform should be controlled under future strategic arms agreements.

Implications for the Air Force

Throughout the Cold War, the U.S. Air Force was a principal source of detailed understanding of the traits of the Soviet military as an opponent. At one level, this corresponded to the creation of specialized knowledge in reports and databases, but more significantly it corresponded to the creation of a body of uniformed specialists—primarily

---

[6] The U.S. does not currently deploy the TLAM-N (since 1992), the only U.S. weapon that is classified as an SLCM in the meaning of the START understanding, although some weapons are retained in storage. Some claim that the TLAM-N has a significant role in extended deterrence in the Pacific. See Congressional Commission on the Strategic Posture of the United States, *America's Strategic Posture: The Final Report of the Congressional Commission on the Strategic Posture of the United States*, Washington, D.C.: United States Institute of Peace, 2009. The purported importance of the TLAM-N to Japan has since been denied by the Japanese government.

intelligence officers, but others as well—who were steeped in the operational practices of their Soviet adversaries as a result of daily observation of Soviet practices in peace, war, and exercises. At the theater level, these specialists and their counterparts in the other services were confident that they could recognize "what comes next" and inform senior military and political leaders as conflict situations developed.

In any possible future conflict involving Russia, American military and political leaders will have a need for deep understanding of potential Russian action. These situations will be fraught with danger precisely because of their novelty and the scarcity of relevant experience. The Air Force must prepare a cadre that is capable of anticipating "what comes next" in a European scenario involving Russia in complicated ways, with multiple levels of force commitment and, ultimately, the potential use of nuclear weapons. This does not imply adding more personnel, but merely that the personnel responsible for planning and operating in such a situation should be fully prepared for the task at hand. Ensuring that they have appropriate training and access to the necessary information (and, indeed, that this information exists, given the limited quality of attention now paid to such issues by both the intelligence community and nongovernment analytical organizations) is the crucial element.

An Air Force aware of these issues will be more effective in contributing to U.S. government deliberations and planning to help prevent inadvertent escalation of conflict to a point where nuclear use becomes a possibility (particularly in situations where Russia might perceive a threat to itself or its allies). This should be a priority for many reasons, not least of which is the fact that—as a primary element of the current American way of war and, from the Russian perspective, the principal component of the American reconnaissance-strike complex—the United States Air Force should expect to be a target of any Russian use of nuclear weapon use in-theater, should this emerge as a real possibility. If averting such situations fails, there are, of course, implications for the operations of the force.

Force planning and deployment basing for operations in Europe need therefore to consider potential nuclear attack on key facilities or functions for waging precision aerial attack. Across the entire range of operations from Kosovo through today, the Russians have been more interested in watching us than we have been interested in watching them, so American planners should not presume that any American-Russian conflict would start with both sides in ignorance. To the extent that Air Force success in the conventional precision-attack mission relies on a small number of known, fixed locations, it invites (and, indeed, may make strategically necessary for the opponent) nuclear attacks that might involve a small number of weapons but greatly compromise the ability to wage an air campaign.

Just as in the Cold War, the potential use of nuclear weapons renders fixed command posts vulnerable and highlights the importance of continuity of command under nuclear attack. The peacetime attraction of isolated facilities, such as command posts and weapon storage (particularly nuclear weapon storage) facilities, becomes a wartime liability in the face of an opponent seeking target sets with large effects and low collateral casualties. Realistic planning should not rely on the survival of such assets.

Operations under a nuclear shadow require many of the same responses proposed for an adversary with highly accurate in-theater resources, with the added requirement to seek to deter, prevent, or otherwise avoid the use of those resources. Reducing the in-theater footprint by exploiting the range of Air Force systems for precision attack and transitioning to long endurance reduces the adversary's perception that small attacks can by themselves change the battlefield outcome. Continental United States (CONUS)–based intelligence and surveillance assets will permit the Air Force to ensure its ability to produce in-theater effects with reduced exposure to in-theater attack. Dispersing in-theater assets across multiple locations and demonstrating independence of peacetime operating locations (as well as main facilities used to support past low-threat operations) also reduces the adversary's assurance that small attacks can significantly affect wartime operations. At the same time, ensuring information connectivity of tactical assets in a nuclear environment would become both more important and more difficult.

In addition to ensuring a capacity to sustain conventional precision-strike operations while under nuclear attack, the Air Force may have to support theater nuclear operations as retaliation or in response to Russian theater nuclear attacks. Any such attacks will originate in conditions quite different from the Cold War NATO nuclear options. Without prejudging NATO decisionmaking on such matters, we note that the changed military geography of Europe discounts the value of past tactical theater-based delivery systems and highlights the capabilities of long-range, CONUS-based Air Force strategic systems.

References

Akhmerov, Evgenii, Oleg Bogdanov, and Marat Valeev, "Neobkhdimosti v Zenitnom Raketnom Prikrytii RVSN Net," *Vozdushno-kosmicheskaia Oborona*, No. 3, 2009.

Arbatov, Alexei, and Vladimir Dvorkin, "Nuclear Deterrence: History, Current State, and Future Prospects," in Alexei Arbatov and Vladimir Dvorkin, eds., *Nuclear Weapons After the Cold War*, Carnegie Moscow Center, Moscow: R. Elinin Publishing House, 2008.

Associated Press, "Russia Says Could Use Nuclear Weapons," January 20, 2008.

Baranets, Viktor, "Pochemu Rossiiskoi Armii Ne Khvataet Novogo Oruzhiia?" *Komsomol'skaia Pravda*, June 18, 2009.

Barsukov, Iurii, "Minoborony Poluchilo Novuiu Tekhniku," *Infox.ru Novie Novosti*, June 17, 2009.

BBC Monitoring, "Russian Strategic Missile Troops General Details Re-Armament, Structure," Ekho Moskvy Radio, September 5, 2009.

Belov, Sergei, "Atom Sderzhivaniia," *Rossiiskaia Gazeta*, March 31, 2006. (Author's translation of Putin statement.)

Blank, Stephen J., *The NATO-Russia Partnership: A Marriage of Convenience or a Troubled Relationship?* Carlisle, Pa.: Strategic Studies Institute, 2006.

Borzov, Arkadii, "VKO: Pora Prekratit' Terminologicheskie Diskussii," *Vozdushno-Kosmicheskaia Oborona*, No. 4, 2010.

Bulavinov, Ilya, *KommersantDdaily*, July 3, 1999.

Central Intelligence Agency, *Implications of Recent Soviet Military-Political Activities*, SNIE 11-10-84, May 11, 1984.

"Chereda Bol'shikh Uchenii," *Argumenty Nedeli*, June 10, 2009.

"Chislo Submarin Tipa 'Iurii Dolgorukii' Budet Zaviset' ot Finansirovaniia," *Lenta.ru*, June 3, 2009. As of February 25, 2011:
http://www.lenta.ru/news/2009/06/03/submarines

Congressional Commission on the Strategic Posture of the United States, *America's Strategic Posture: The Final Report of the Congressional Commission on the Strategic Posture of the United States*, Washington, D.C.: United States Institute of Peace, 2009.

"Dal'niaia Aviatsiia Zamenit Tu-160 i Tu-22M3 Novym Bombardirovshchikom," *Lenta.ru*, December 12, 2009.

Day, Matthew, "Russia 'Simulates' Nuclear Attack on Poland," *Telegraph.co.uk*, November 1, 2009. As of February 25, 2011: http://www.telegraph.co.uk/news/worldnews/europe/poland/6480227/Russia-simulates-nuclear-attack-on-Poland.html

Dubrov, V., "Aviation in Local Wars: In Search of New Tactics," *Aviatsiia i Kosmonautika*, October 1991, translated in JPRS-UAC-92-005, May 4, 1992.

Dunin, Anna, "Intel Brief: Poland on Edge over Russian Drills," International Relations and Security Network, November 18, 2009. As of September 26, 2010: http://www.isn.ethz.ch/isn/Current-Affairs/Security-Watch/Detail/?id=109702&lng=en

Ermarth, Fritz W., "Observations on the 'War Scare' of 1983 from an Intelligence Perch," Parallel History Project on NATO and the Warsaw Pact, Stasi Intelligence on NATO, edited by Bernd Schaefer and Christian Nuenlist, November 6, 2003. As of February 25, 2011: http://php.isn.ethz.ch/collections/colltopic.cfm?lng=en&id=17325&navinfo=15296

Erokhin, I. V., "Kakie Vooruzhennye Sily Nuzhny Rossii," *Voennaia Mysl*, No. 4, April 2009.

Esin, Viktor, "SShA: Kurs Na Global'nuyu PRO," *Voenno-Promyshlennyi Kur'er*, No. 33, August 31, 2010.

Falichev, Egor Sozaev-Gur'ev, "Kazaki I Raketchiki Protiv 'Bangrupy,'" *Infox.ru*, July 8, 2010. As of February 25, 2011: http://infox.ru/authority/defence/2010/07/07/Kazaki_i_rakyetchiki.phtml

Falichev, Oleg, "'Vostok-2010': Nachalo, Kul'minatsiia, Epilog," *Voenno-Promyshlennyi Kur'er*, July 14, 2010.

Fedorov, Andrei, "Novoe Prishestvie 'Satany,'" *Lenta.ru*, June 12, 2009. As of February 25, 2011: http://www.lenta.ru/articles/2009/06/12/satan/

Freedman, Lawrence, *The Evolution of Nuclear Strategy*, 3rd ed., New York: Palgrave Macmillan, 2003.

———, *Deterrence*, Cambridge, UK: Polity Press, 2004.

Gareev, M. A., "Problemy Strategicheskogo Sderzhivaniia v Sovermennykh Usloviiakh," *Voennaia Mysl*, No. 4, April 2009.

Gareev, M. A., and I. V. Erokhin, "Kakie Vooruzhennye Sily Nuzhny Rossii," *Voennaia Mysl*, No. 4, April 2009.

Gates, Robert M., *From the Shadows: The Ultimate Insider's Story of Five Presidents and How They Won the Cold War*, New York: Simon & Schuster, 1996.

Glaser, Charles L., "Why Do Strategists Disagree About the Requirements of Strategic Nuclear Deterrence?" in Lynn Eden and Steven E. Miller, eds., *Nuclear Arguments: Understanding the Strategic Nuclear Arms and Arms Control Debates*, Ithaca, N.Y.: Cornell University Press, 1989.

Golos Rosii, "RVSN Provodiat IAdernye Ucheniia," March 10, 2010.

"Golovami Otvetiat," *Vzgliad*, April 10, 2009.

Gottemoeller, Rose E., *Land-Attack Cruise Missiles*, London: International Institute for Strategic Studies, 1987.

Gottemoeller, Rose, "Nuclear Necessity in Putin's Russia," *Arms Control Today*, April 2004.

Halpin, Tony, "Russia to Test Fire Cruise Missiles for First Time Since 1984," *Times Online*, October 6, 2008. As of February 25, 2011:
http://www.timesonline.co.uk/tol/news/world/europe/article4891656.ece

Hines, John G., Ellis M. Mishulovich, and John F. Shull, *Soviet Intentions 1965–1985*, Volume I: *An Analytical Comparison of U.S.-Soviet Assessments During the Cold War*, McLean, Va.: BDM Federal, Inc., September 1995.

Hoffman, David E., *The Dead Hand: The Untold Story of the Cold War Arms Race and Its Dangerous Legacy*, New York: Doubleday, 2009.

"Ispytaniia 'Bulavy' Prodolzhatsia," *Voenno-Promyshlennyi Kur'er*, No. 28, July 22, 2009.

"Ispytaniia 'Bulavy' Vozobnoviatsia do Kontsa Mesiatsa," *RIA Novosti*, September 8, 2010.

Ivashov, Leonid, "Politicheskaya Tsena Iadernoi' Bomby," *Nezavisimoe Voennoe Obozrenie*, No. 19, June 5, 2009a.

Ivashov, Leonid Grigor'evich, "Podozritel'naia Speshka v Sokrashchenii IAdernikh Vooruzhenii," *Nezavisimaia Gazeta*, July 6, 2009b.

Kartchner, Kerry M., *Negotiating START: The Quest for Stability and the Making of the Strategic Arms Reduction Treaty*, New Brunswick, N.J.: Transaction, 1992.

Kazennov, Sergei, and Vladimir Kumachev, "Ne Nado Absoliutizirovat' 'Ugrozu S Vostoka," *Nezavisimoe Voennoe Obozrenie*, No. 30, August 13, 2010.

Khramchikhin, Aleksandr, "Smes' Iz Kompleksov, Samoobmana I Obmana," *Nezavisimoe Voennoe Obozrenie*, No. 18, May 29, 2009a.

———, "VMF RF Na Zarubezhnikh Korabliakh," *Nezavisimoe Voennoe Obozrenie,* July 3, 2009b.

———, "Starye Osnovy Novoi Doktriny," *Voenno-Promyshlennyi Kur'er,* No. 6, February 17, 2010a.

———, "Illiuziia IAdernogo Sderzhivaniia," *Voenno-Promyshlennyi Kur'er,* No. 11, March 24, 2010b.

———, "Neadekvatnyi Vostok," *Nezavisimoe Voennoe Obozrenie,* No. 27, July 23, 2010c.

Kipp, Jacob W., "Russia's Nonstrategic Nuclear Weapons," *Military Review,* May–June 2001.

Kipp, Jacob W., and Nikolai Sokov, "Chronology of Significant Military Maneuvers," Nuclear Threat Initiative, August 2004. As of February 25, 2011: http://www.nti.org/db/nisprofs/russia/weapons/maneuver.htm

Kirshin, Iurii, "Osnovopolagaiushchie Printsipy Zashchity Strany," *Nezavisimoe Voennoe Obozrenie,* No. 13, April 10, 2009.

Kissinger, Henry, *Diplomacy,* New York: Simon and Schuster, 1994.

KM-Novosti, "Zavodskii Brak Sorval Zapusk 'Bulavi,'" June 3, 2009.

Kokoshin, Andrei, *Strategicheskoe Upravlenie: Teoria, Istoricheskiy Opyt, Sravnitel'ny Analiz, Zadachi Dlia Rossii,* Moscow: MGIMO Press, ROSSPEN Publishers, 2003.

———, "'Assimmetrichnyi Otvet' vs. 'Strategicheskoi Oboronnoi Initsiativy,'" *Mezhdunarodnaia Zhizn',* No. 7, August 2007.

"Konstruktor 'Bulavi' Podal v Otstavku Iz-Za Neudachnogo Puska Rakety," *Lenta.ru,* July 22, 2009. As of February 25, 2011: http://www.lenta.ru/news/2009/07/22/resign

Korotchenko, Igor', "Sokhranit' Potentsial Otvetnogo Udara," *Voenno-Promyshlennyi Kur'er,* No. 20, May 27, 2009.

———, "SNV, PRO i Budushchee Rosiiskikh Strategicheskikh IAdernykh Sil," *Natsional'naia Oborona,* No. 4, April 2010.

Kozhukin, Matvei, "Iadernoe Oruzhie—Faktor Sderzhivaniia," *Krasnaia Zvezda,* February 10, 2010.

Kozin, Vladimir, "IAdernye Dilemmy," *Krasnaia Zvezda,* No. 90, May 22, 2009.

———, "Novaia IAdernaia Doktrina SSHA: Anakhronism Sokhraniaetsia," *Natsional'naia Oborona,* No. 4, April 2010.

Kramnik, Il'ia, "Razmakh Vpechatliaet, A Problemy Trevozhat," *Voenno-Promyshlennyi Kur'er,* July 13, 2010.

Lavrov, Sergei, "Novyi Dogovor o SNV v Matritse Global'noi Bezopasnosti," *Mezhdunarodnaia Zhizn'*, No. 7, July 2010.

Levshin, V. I., A. V. Nedelin, and M. E. Sosnovsky, "O Primenenii IAdernogo Oruzhiia Dlia Deeskalatsii Voennykh Deistvii [On Employing Nuclear Weapons to De-Escalate Military Operations]," *Voyennaya Mysl [Journal of Military Thought: A Russian Journal of Military Theory and Strategy]*, May–June 1999, pp. 34–37.

Lieber, Keir A., and Daryl G. Press , "The End of MAD: The Nuclear Dimension of U.S. Primacy," *International Security*, Vol. 30, No. 4, Spring 2006a.

———, "The Rise of U.S. Nuclear Primacy," *Foreign Affairs*, Vol. 85, No. 2, March–April 2006b.

Lubold, Gordon, "Why U.S.-Poland Missile Deal Rouses Russian Bear," *Christian Science Monitor*, August 19, 2008.

Lutovinov, Vladimir, "Sistema Voennykh Ugroz Bezopasnosti Rossii: Voenno-Politicheskii Analiz," *Voennye Znaniia*, No. 1, January 2009.

"L'vinaia Dolia Biudzheta MO Idet VMF, v Ocnovnom IAdernym Silam—Ivanov," *RIA Novosti*, June 3, 2009.

Malyshev, Vladlen, and E'duard Bogatyriev, "Voennye Ugrozy I Ikh Vliianie na Planirovanie Mereopriiatii Grazhdanskoi Oborony," *Voennye Znaniia*, No. 5, May 2009.

Mamlyga, Vadim, "Ucheniia V Gruzii: Chto Za Factom? Igra Na Vyzhivanie," *Flag Rodiny*, No. 94, June 2, 2009.

Mamontov, Vladimir, "Meniaetsia Rossiia, Meniaetsia i Ee Voennaia Doktrina," *Izvestiia*, October 14, 2009.

Mankoff, Jeffrey, *Russian Foreign Policy: The Return of Great Power Politics*, Lanham, Md.: Rowman & Littlefield, 2009.

Maruev, A. IU., "Voennye Aspekty Formirovaniia Geopoliticheskikh Interesov I Geostrategii Rosii," *Voennaia Mysl*, No. 1, January 2009.

Matvichuk, V. V., and A. L. Khriapkin, "Sistema Strategicheskogo Sderzhivaniia v Novykh Usloviiakh," *Voennaia Mysl*, No. 1, January 2010.

McDermott, Roger, "*Zapad 2009* Rehearses Countering a NATO Attack on Belarus," *Jamestown Foundation Eurasia Daily Monitor*, Vol. 6, No. 179, September 30, 2009.

Medvedev, Dmitry, "Opening Address at a Meeting with Commanders of Military Districts," September 26, 2008. As of February 25, 2011: http://www.kremlin.ru/eng/speeches/2008/09/26/2019_type82912type84779_206970.shtml

————, "Interview Given by Dmitry Medvedev to Television Channels Channel One, Rossia, NTV," August 31, 2008. As of February 25, 2011: http://www.kremlin.ru/eng/speeches/2008/08/31/1850_type82912type82916_206003.shtml

Medvedev, Dmitry, and Barack Obama, "Treaty Between the United States of America and the Russian Federation on Measures for the Further Reduction and Limitation of Strategic Offensive Arms," signed April 8, 2010. As of February 25, 2011: http://www.state.gov/documents/organization/140035.pdf

Miasnikov, Viktor, "Ispytaniia 'Bulavy': Opiat' Samolikvidatziia," *Nezavisimaia Gazeta*, July 17, 2009.

Morozov, Igor, Sergei Baushev, and Oleg Kaminskii, "Kosmos i Kharakter Sovremennykh Voennykh Deistvii," *Vozdushno-kosmicheskaia Oborona*, No. 4, 2009.

"Nachal'nik Genshtaba VS RF Nikolai Makarov: 'Bulava' Dolzhna Poletet," *Nauka I Tekhnologii Rossii—STRF.ru*, June 16, 2009.

National Security Council of Russia, "Voennaia Doktrina Rossiiskoi Federatsii," Presidential Ukaz No. 706, April 21, 2000. As of February 25, 2011: http://www.scrf.gov.ru/documents/33.html

————, "Strategiia Natzional'noi Bezopasnosti Rossiiskoi Federatsii do 2020 Goda," Presidential Ukaz No. 537, May 12, 2009. As of February 25, 2011: http://www.scrf.gov.ru/documents/99.html
English-language version available, as of February 25, 2011, at: http://www.carnegieendowment.org/files/2010russia_military_doctrine.pdf

————, "Voennaia Doktrina Rossiiskoi Federatsii," February 5, 2010. As of February 25, 2011: http://news.kremlin.ru/ref_notes/461

Nesterov, Sergei, and Sergei Volkov, "Eshche Raz o Sisteme VKO," *Vozdushno-Kosmicheskaia Oborona*, No. 4, 2010.

News Detail, "The Russian Armed Forces Began the Stability-2008 Strategic Command and Staff Exercises," Moscow, September 22, 2008.

"Novosti v Rosii," *Vozdushno-Kosmicheskaia Oborona*, No. 1, 2009a.

"Novosti v Rosii," *Vozdushno-Kosmicheskaia Oborona*, No. 3, 2009b.

Office of the Secretary of Defense, *Report of the Secretary of Defense Task Force on DoD Nuclear Weapons Management: Phase II: Review of the DoD Nuclear Mission*, Washington, D.C., December 2008. As of February 25, 2011: http://www.defense.gov/pubs/pdfs/PhaseIIReportFinal.pdf

Oliker, Olga, Keith Crane, Lowell H. Schwartz, and Catherine Yusupov, *Russian Foreign Policy: Sources and Implications*, Santa Monica, Calif.: RAND Corporation, MG-768-AF, 2009. As of February 25, 2011:
http://www.rand.org/pubs/monographs/MG768.html

"Only 8 Russian Strategic Submarines Are Combat-Ready—Analyst," *Johnson's Russia List*, No. 101, June 1, 2009, citing *RIA Novosti*.

Organization for Security and Co-operation in Europe, *Vienna Document 1999: Of the Negotiations on Confidence- and Security-Building Measures*, November 1999. As of February 25, 2011:
http://www.osce.org/fsc/41276

Permanent Representation of the Russian Federation to the Council of Europe, "2000 Russian National Security Concept" (English version), 2000. As of February 25, 2011:
http://www.russiaeurope.mid.ru/russiastrat2000.html

"Perviy Division Raket RS-24 Zastupil na Boevoe Dezhurstvo v RF," *RIA Novosti*, July 19, 2010.

Pinchuk, Aleksandr, "Obshchestvennyi Sovet—Na Baze RVSN," *Krasnaia Zvezda*, No. 105, June 17, 2009.

Podvig, Paul, ed., *Russian Strategic Nuclear Forces,* Cambridge, Mass.: MIT Press, 2004.

———, "Speaking of Nuclear Primacy," Russian Strategic Nuclear Forces website (russianforces.org), March 10, 2006a. As of February 25, 2011:
http://russianforces.org/blog/2006/03/speaking_of_nuclear_primacy.shtml

———, "Russia Discusses Nuclear Weapons," Russian Strategic Nuclear Forces website (russianforces.org), March 31, 2006b. As of February 25, 2011:
http://russianforces.org/blog/2006/03/russia_discusses_nuclear_weapo.shtml

———, "Nuclear Primacy Again," Russian Strategic Nuclear Forces website (russianforces.org), August 22, 2006c. As of February 25, 2011:
http://russianforces.org/blog/2006/08/nuclear_primacy_again.shtml

———, "Ten Missile Submarine Patrols in 2008," Russian Strategic Nuclear Forces website (russianforces.org), February 17, 2008a. As of February 25, 2011:
http://www.russianforces.org/blog/2009/02/ten_missile_submarine_patrols.shtml

———, "Tu-160 Modernization Program Is Underway," Russian Strategic Nuclear Forces website (russianforces.org), April 26, 2008b. As of February 25, 2011:
http://www.russianforces.org/blog/2008/04/tu160_modernization_program_is.shtml

————, "Russia Added New Tu-160 to Its Bomber Force," Russian Strategic Nuclear Forces website (russianforces.org), April 28, 2008c. As of February 25, 2011:
http://www.russianforces.org/blog/2008/04/Russia_added_new_tu160_to_its.shtml

————, "Tu-95 MS Go Through Modernization," Russian Strategic Nuclear Forces website (russianforces.org), July 5, 2008d. As of February 25, 2011:
http://www.russianforces.org/blog/2008/07/tu-95ms_go_through_modernizati.shtml

————, "Strategic Aviation," Russian Strategic Nuclear Forces website (russianforces.org), April 3, 2009a. As of February 25, 2011:
http://www.russianforces.org/aviation/

————, "Rocket Forces Tell About Plans for 2009," Russian Strategic Nuclear Forces website (russianforces.org), April 10, 2009b. As of February 25, 2011:
http://www.russianforces.org/blog/2009/04/rocket_forces_tell_about_plans.shtml

————, "Stealth Plans," Russian Strategic Nuclear Forces website (russianforces.org), December 22, 2009c. As of February 25, 2011:
http://www.russianforces.org/blog/2009/12/stealth_plans.shtml

————, "Second Topol-M Regiment in Teykovo," Russian Strategic Nuclear Forces website (russianforces.org), March 1, 2010a. As of February 25, 2011:
http://www.russianforces.org/blog/2010/03/second_topol-m_regiment_in_tey.shtml

————, "Le RS-24 Est Arrivé," blog post, Russian Strategic Nuclear Forces website (russianforces.org), July 19, 2010b. As of February 25, 2011:
http://www.russianforces.org/blog/2010/07/le_rs-24_est_arriv.shtml

————, "Early Warning," Russian Strategic Nuclear Forces website (russianforces.org), updated September 2, 2010c. As of February 25, 2011:
http://www.russianforces.org/sprn

President of Russia, website, 2011. As of February 28, 2011:
http://eng.kremlin.ru/

Press Center of Nuclear Energy and Industry, "Dmitry Medvedev Zaiavliaet o Neobkhodimosti Povisheniia Boegotovnosti Iadernikh Sil RF," citing *Interfax,* March 18, 2009. As of February 25, 2011:
http://www.minatom.ru/news/14218_18.03.2009

Protasov, A. A., S. V. Kreidin, and S. IU. Egorov, "Sistemy Upravleniia Voiskami (Silami) Kak Instrument Strategicheskogo Sderzhivaniia," *Voennaia Mysl,* No. 7, July 2009.

Quinlivan, James T., "Soviet Air and Air Defense Forces and Their Successors, Lessons from the Gulf War," in Theodore W. Karasik, *Russia and Eurasia Armed Forces Review Annual, Volume 15—1991,* Gulf Breeze, Fl.: Academic International Press, 1999.

"RF Budet Uvelichivat' Rol' Takticheskogo Iadernogo Oruzhiia Na Mnogotselevykh APL," *Gazeta* (gzt.ru), March 23, 2009.

Rogov, Sergei, Pavel Zolatarev, Viktor Esin, and Valerii Iarynich, "Sud'ba Strategicheskikh Vooruzhenii Posle Pragi," *Nezavisimoe Voennoe Obozrenie,* No. 32, August 27, 2010.

"Rossiiskoe Iadernoe Oruzhie: Kriterii Primeneniia," *Natsional'naia Oborona,* No. 2, February 2010.

Ruchkin, Viktor, "V Poiskakh Paradigmy Stabil'nosti," *Krasnaia Zvezda,* No. 68, April 16, 2009.

"Russia to Conduct Large-Scale War Games in the Fall," *RIA Novosti,* March 10, 2009. As of February 28, 2011:
http://www.en.rian.ru/russia/20090310/120498364.html

"Russian, Belarusian Leaders to Discuss Trade, Military Ties," *RIA Novosti,* September 29, 2009. As of February 28, 2011:
http://en.rian.ru/russia/20090929/156282585.html

"Russian Bombers Test High-Precision Weaponry During Drills," *RIA Novosti,* September 27, 2009. As of February 28, 2011: http://en.rian.ru/mlitary_news/20090928/156269949.html

"Russian Chief of Staff Warns Against NATO Expansion," *Georgian Daily,* April 11, 2008.

Russian Ministry of Defence, website, no date-a. As of February 28, 2011:
http://www.mil.ru/eng/

———, "Mission," no date-b. As of February 28, 2011:
http://www.mil.ru/eng/1862/12068/12090/index.shtml

———, "Press-Reliz Ob'edinennogo Press-Tsentra Operativno-Strategicheskogo Ucheniia 'Zapad-2009,'" September 29, 2009a.

———, "Press Release of the Incorporated Press Centre of the Operative-and-Strategic Exercise 'Zapad-2009' ('West-2009')," September 30, 2009b.

"Russia's Strategic Missile Forces to Play War Games on Sept. 8–11," *RIA Novosti,* September 7, 2009. As of February 28, 2011:
http://en.rian.ru/mlitary_news/20090907/156052331.html

"RVSN Osnashchaiutsia Novymi Raketami s Razdeliaiushchimisia Boegolovkami," *ARMS TASS,* September 7, 2009.

"RVSN Perevooruzhaiutsia," *Nezavisimoe Voennoe Obozrenie,* June 16, 2009a.

"RVSN Perevooruzhaiutsia," *Vozdushno-Kosmicheskaia Oborona*, No. 3, 2009b.

"RVSN Segodnia i Zavtra," *Voenno-Promyshlennyi Kur'er*, April 22, 2009.

"Serdiukov Ne Velel Ustraivat' Voinu Dvukh Armii," *Nezavisimoe Voennoe Obozrenie*, July 9, 2010.

Sirotinin, E. S., "Sderzhivanie Agressii v Kontekste Novoi Voennoi Doktriny Rossiiskoi Federatsii," *Voennaia Mysl*, No. 5, May 2010.

Slipchenko, Vladimir I., "Russian Analysis of Warfare Leading to the Sixth Generation," *Field Artillery*, October 1993.

———, *Bezkontaktnye Voiny*, Moscow: Gran Press, 2001.

Slipchenko, Vladimir I., and M. A. Gareev, *Voina Budushchego: Shestoe Pokolenie*, Moscow: Mosckovskiy Obshchestvenniy Nauchniy Fond, 1999.

Sokov, Nikolai, "Military Exercise in Russia: Naval Deterrence Failures Compensated by Strategic Rocket Success," Center for Nonproliferation Studies Research Story, Monterey Institute of International Studies, February 24, 2004. As February 28, 2011: http://cns.miis.edu/stories/040224.htm

Solov'ev, Vadim, "Strategiia—Novaia, Podkhody—Konservativnye," *Nezavisimoe Voennoe Obozrenie*, No. 17, May 22, 2009.

Sukhanov, Sergei, "VKOEto Zadacha, a Ne Sistema," *Vozdushno-Kosmicheskaia Oborona*, No. 2, 2010.

Suri, Jeremy, "Explaining the End of the Cold War: A New Historical Consensus," *Journal of Cold War Studies*, Vol. 4, No. 4, Fall 2002.

Troitskii, Kirill, "Vo Imia 'Global'nogo Poriadka?'" *Voenno-Promyshlennyi Kur'er*, No. 20, May 27, 2009.

"Ucheniia 'Zapad-2009': Rossiiskie Raketonostzy Pribyli v Belorussiiu," *Zvezdanews*, September 23, 2009.

U.S. Congress, 102nd Cong., 1st Session, "Message from the President of the U.S. Transmitting the START Treaty, Signed at Moscow on July 31, 1991, Including the Treaty Text, Annexes on Agreed Statements and Definitions, Protocols on Conversion or Elimination, Inspections, Notifications, Throw-Weight, Telemetry, JCIC, and the MOU," U.S. Senate Treaty Doc. 102-20, November 25, 1991.

Usol'tsev, Valerii, "Boi Na Sergeevskom Poligone," *Suvorovskii Natisk*, July 17, 2010.

"V Podmoskov'e Proidut Ucheniia Protivodiversionnoi Roty RVSN," *Oruzhie Rosii*, July 14, 2008.

"V Ucheniiakh 'Vostok-2010' Primut Uchastie Kosmicheskie Voiska i RVSN," *RIA Novosti,* June 28, 2010.

Vadim Solov'ev, "Strategiia—Novaia, Podkhody—Konservativnye," *Nezavisimoe Voennoe Obozrenie*, No. 17, May 22, 2009.

"Vazhnyi Etap 'Aleksandra Nevskogo,'" *Korabel*, June 16, 2009.

Viatkin, IAroslav, "Chereda Bol'shikh Uchenii," Argumenty Nedeli, July 10, 2009.

Weitz, Richard, *Russian-American Security Cooperation After St. Petersburg: Challenges and Opportunities*, Carlisle, Pa.: Strategic Studies Institute, 2007.

Yost, David S., "Russia's Non-Strategic Nuclear Forces," *International Affairs*, Vol. 77, No. 3, July 2001, pp. 531–551.

Zaitsev, Yuri, "Bulava-M: Still Far from Flying," *RIA Novosti*, September 8, 2005.

"Zakladka Chetvertoi APL 'Borei' Perenositsia na Pervii Kvartal 2010 Goda," *RIA Novosti*, December 15, 2009.